SECOND THOUGHTS

Books by Brian Masters

Molière

Sartre

Saint-Exupéry

Rabelais

Camus

Wynyard Hall and the Londonderry Family

Dreams about H. M. The Queen

The Dukes

Now Barabbas Was a Rotter: The Extraordinary Life of Marie Corelli

The Mistresses of Charles II

Georgiana, Duchess of Devonshire

Great Hostesses

Killing for Company: The Case of Dennis Nilsen

The Swinging Sixties

The Passion of John Aspinall

Maharana: The Udaipur Dynasty

Gary

The Life of E. F. Benson

Voltaire's Treatise on Tolerance (edited and translated)

The Shrine of Jeffrey Dahmer

Masters on Murder

The Evil That Men Do

'She Must Have Known': The Trial of Rosemary West

Thunder in the Air: Great Actors in Great Roles

Getting Personal: A Biographer's Memoir

Second Thoughts

BRIAN MASTERS

First published in 2008 by
Quartet Books Limited
A member of the Namara Group
27 Goodge Street, London W1T 2LD

A catalogue record for this book
is available from the British Library

ISBN   978 0 7043 7140 8

Typeset by Antony Gray
Printed and bound in Great Britain by
T J International Ltd, Padstow, Cornwall

FOR
Anurag Samuel
'Lucky'

Preface

This is in essence a postscript to *Getting Personal*, but it makes no attempt to be chronological. There were events, portraits and reflections which could not easily find a place in that book, thereby leaving gaps which needed to be filled. This, I hope, fills some of the gaps, but the chapters are necessarily episodic and discursive, meandering in allusive mode across a lifetime of incident and encounter. If there be any thread which ties them, it is a sense of delight that I have been able to emerge from the gloom of wartime London and benefit so widely from the opportunities offered me by an insatiable curiosity.

Castries, France, 2008

CHAPTER ONE

Some People and an Insult

My living in this house in the South of France is almost entirely an accident. And yet I feel, not with conviction (for feelings are irrational) but with a nervous certainty, that the house called me. While I most definitely was not looking for it, it, I am sure, was looking for me.

Because it is tucked away in the corner of a square in the centre of the village, one may pass the house and not see it. Indeed, I must have done so many times, for I lived in another house a hundred yards away, in the shadow of the castle, once the grand seat of the Duc de Castries, now still imposing but empty, brooding goliath-like on the top of the hill and visible for miles around. One other point in the village is also discernible from afar, the nineteenth-century church steeple, only slightly less lofty than the massive castle. I am now next to that. So I have swapped one shadow for another.

My old house was a twelfth-century wonder, snuggling up against the walls of the castle and slightly underground. With vaulted stone rooms, a spiral staircase up into the air, and drainage built by the Romans, it was obviously not meant to be a house at all, but had probably been part of the underground rooms of the ancient mediaeval castle which predated the present one. Neighbours remember it as a chicken-house only fifty years ago. If one may imagine oneself living with the wine-bottles and spiders in the cellar of the Tower of London, one may have an approximate idea of the romance of the place, as well as its inconvenience. Damp was never entirely

11

conquered, even in this dry climate, and the stones of the ceiling daily dropped their dust into one's porridge. The damp, I discovered, arose from the occasional torrential rainwaters which were directed off the castle grounds into the next Roman well down the hill, which was outside my door. The well filled up from below, but not before its waters had flowed through my drawing-room.

Nevertheless, No 1 rue du Quartier Bas had its unique cachet and I felt terribly historical living within its walls. The vaults were the largest in the village, the flagstone floors the most extensive and perfect.

One Sunday morning I walked along the narrow mediaeval street which borders the castle wall and opens up into broader skies above and around the church. Just past the church is the Place Emile Granier, named, as I later found out, after one of the only three villagers who did not embrace the German conquerors in 1940 and who subsequently perished for his patriotism in Auschwitz. In one of the houses of this square lives Guy, Emile Granier's nephew. There were two other houses, one let to the Clermond family, the other a nest of small apartments. And then the big iron gates in the corner, which I had not noticed before.

I peered through them. Behind was a triangular courtyard, weed-infested and grim, and beyond that the doors of what I surmised was a garage, above the garage a terrace, which descended to the courtyard by a stone stairway to the right, and on the left turned at right-angles. So the house was L-shaped, with rooms above the terrace in front of me, and to the left of me. The walls were covered in boring cement, the terrace itself virtually hidden by a vine which had been left to grow berserk, choking all view of any windows. I could see enough, however, to notice that the shutters were all closed. Both doors at ground-level, in the old Languedoc style each with a huge outside bolt stretching right across the width of the door, were likewise closed and silent. It was pretty obvious that the house had been, if not abandoned, then certainly left to take care of itself. It looked temporarily forgotten, and I was curious. There was not a clue as to what might lie behind the walls. It could not be much, I was tempted to think.

I went to the local estate agent at the bottom of the village and made enquiries. Sure enough, the house was for sale, and an offer had been made and accepted. The agent was sufficiently indiscreet to admit that it had taken a long time to dispose of that particular house. One academic gentleman had been interested a few months before, but had backed out when he heard the church bells next door. It appears that many people do not care for the sound of church bells, a discovery which perplexed me. It was now being bought by a Belgian, who intended to convert it into a lodging-house. Meanwhile, there could be no objection to my taking a look, even though nothing to my advantage would ensue.

So I took the keys, with the name 'Roux' written on the tab, and walked back up the hill to Place Emile Granier, and thus did I make my first acquaintance with No 6, as one might cautiously pluck up courage to ask for a date. I stepped gingerly within, and paused politely. I felt I was drawing aside a veil which the house had itself kept in place for self-protection.

It was certainly gloomy. The first floor, with the terrace, had a bourgeois dining-room, with heavy dark table and six plastic-seated chairs, a television set in the corner, a sunken leather-bound armchair, and a sideboard. The fireplace was grey flecked granite. Adjacent to this was a makeshift kitchen, with sink in the far corner, cooker next to it, plastic cupboard for cups and saucers and a little table by the window with two chairs. The floors of both these rooms were miserable fake teracotta tiles. Also on this floor were three bedrooms, in one of which was a nineteenth-century French wooden bed and wardrobe, which looked as if they had been there longer than the house itself, the walls having risen around them. The wardrobe was packed with hand-made curtains, bedspreads, table-runners, napkins, and a pile of nineteenth-century embroidered linen night-dresses, obviously some sort of trousseau which was still waiting to be unfolded. In a drawer of the wardrobe were a widow's mourning-weeds, and a rosary and prayer-book. And on the dressing-table beneath the window were a pair of old lady's round spectacles, and three gentleman's cut-throat razors.

The floors of all three rooms were made of magnificent *dalles*, heavy square flag-stones of a kind now difficult to find and impossible to afford. And when I looked up at the ceilings, I saw they were solid, peasant, devoid of ornament but abounding in that simple dignity which good craftsmen manage to impose upon necessity; the joists holding up the floor above were made an attractive feature of the ceilings. This side of the house had evidently not been bourgeois, but was of earlier date. Finally, there was a lavatory and a workroom, with Singer sewing-machine, deep, heavy porcelain sink and pink bathtub.

Up the stone staircase to the floor above revealed another bedroom, which had clearly not been used for ages, and a gigantic attic room, stuffed with everything which had to be placed out of sight for the last hundred years or so – bits of an old iron bedstead, a soldier's First World War trunk and uniform, battered portraits face to the wall, and cobwebs of long endurance. Beneath piles of 1930s newspapers stood an infant's high-chair, and next to it was a child's sloping-lid desk, complete with crayon-box, ruler, and set of geometric devices. One fancied finding Miss Havisham, herself draped and cob-webbed, sitting in the corner.

Back down the stairs and passing the terrace floor, I found another stone staircase descended into yet another magic slice of Time Past, the unused ground floor. Here was a magnificent Languedoc kitchen, with huge open fireplace occupying almost the entirety of one wall, ancient brick and tiled warming-ovens, old scales, the *cafetières* one expects to find in a painting, and a rickety old trestle-table. None of this, it was plain, had been touched for fifty years. Next door was a workshop, with bench, hand-made boxes containing every possible tool, tins with thousands of buttons, and a chest which held several hundred different sizes of nails and screws. There were other tins for hinges, for bolts, for handles, for electrical fittings, for oils, for brushes, for rubber-bands, for strings, for grease, for bells, for keys (each one meticulously labelled), and God knows what else. Whoever had lived here never threw anything away. The house was a curiously self-sufficient treasure-trove, negating any need for shops. On the other side of the old kitchen a door led to a large woodshed, a wine-cellar (still with bottles and casks), and the garage, itself piled with yet more stuff from another life.

It was then that I felt the house speak to me. It asked to be woken up, to be rescued from a coma, and above all to be saved from the fate of destruction and fragmentation which the Belgian had in store for it. But it would take a little while, and some unforeseeable shifts in fate, before I could answer.

I asked the agent if the sale was certain. As far as he knew, I was too late, but he would keep me informed. The price, at over £100,000, would in any case be affordable only if I managed to sell the chicken-coop in which I was living, and this was un-likely, since it had no garage, no garden, nowhere for children to play or for teenagers to rev up their engines; it was fit only for a crusty old bachelor like me. So I secretly sighed with relief that I should not have to declare my love and offer myself. It would have been impossible, or, even worse, possible yet catastrophic.

When, therefore, the estate agent called a few days later to announce that the deal had fallen through, and that the house was once more up for sale, my stomach leapt and shuddered; I suppose that is what is meant by people writing about 'mixed feelings'. I could not resist at least paying a second call, perchance to confirm me in my doubts and reassure me that I should do better to leave well alone. But I did not reckon with the house's resolute need. It was as if I were being grasped in a desperate embrace. I saw at once how the boring bourgeois dining-room and tawdry kitchen next to it could be combined into one well-proportioned sitting-room; indeed, the wall dividing them was not original – it was hollow, and could be removed in a trice. Then the antique kitchen downstairs could be brought back to life with minimum effort – a chimney-clean, replacement of some broken and blackened tiles, a new floor, but essentially retaining its character. It could be used as a dining-room, with a roaring fire boosting the appetite in winter, while the workshop next to it, into which one passed not through a door but under an arch, was the perfect size and position for a modern equipped kitchen. There was scope for much more, and the individual sizes and shapes of the rooms, appearing at surprising intervals and opening into unsuspected spaces, could offer a decorator (namely myself) opportunities for creativity without in any way spoiling the ambiance of the house. The room with bed and wardrobe would become a guest room, and would be home to the old portraits in the attic, so that the original inhabitants could be reunited with their 'things' and the line of history continue through inanimate objects. If such an idea smacked of a dreary museum, I knew that it need not be so.

Scratching a little here and there, I could see that the frightful concrete on the exterior concealed an original stone-built house, its beauty betrayed for who knew how many years.

It appeared that the sale had fallen through because the

Belgian, whom the house obviously distrusted and whom the neighbours had likewise taken umbrage against because he had announced that he would require all their parking-spaces for his tenants, disputed the price at the last minute and attempted to negotiate a reduction. Now this is almost criminal behaviour in France. It is certainly a gross insult. 'Gazumping' is unheard of here; once a price has been agreed, the purchaser signs a *compromis de vente* to which he is thenceforth bound. The vendors likewise cannot break the contract if they get a better offer. Too late! A month or so later, once finance has been arranged, the partners to the agreement – vendor and purchaser – meet before the *notaire* to finalise the arrangement and exchange keys. This is a formal matter, a little like appearing in a registry office, and it terminates with the handing over of keys and the pronouncement of the lawyer that the transfer of ownership has been effected. It was at this (to the French, solemn) ceremony that the Belgian put his foot in it. The vendors stormed out of the office in a huff, and the sale was considered automatically cancelled by the Belgian's *faux pas*.

That is where I came in, both eager and scared. I made an offer twenty-five per cent below the asking-price, which I knew would be unacceptable and would thereby solve my dilemma. Two days later the offer was accepted, and I was captured. I signed the *compromis de vente*.

I soon learned why this house seemed not to have been disturbed for so long, and why it was so keen not to be disturbed now. The owners, Monsieur and Madame Roux, were eighty-six and eighty years old respectively, but they had not lived here in any continuous fashion. Monsieur Roux had been born here, and it was his high-chair and school-desk which lay in the attic covered in years of dust. The soldier's trunk had also been witness to a chapter of his life, and I recognised among the neglected portraits a photograph of a boy aged about eleven, who one could just make out was the same person who was selling me the house. So was it his life that he was bartering away? Not at all. He had left the house as a young man to serve in the military and then to marry, and had naturally moved to his own home some miles away. When his parents died, they left him his childhood home, which he simply took as it was, and visited from time to time, perhaps for a weekend every couple of months, or for a week or two in the sultry summer. Monsieur Roux was selling not *his* house, but *his parents'* house. I was skipping a generation, and the presence of the parents was still more palpable in this place than the faint impression made by their son's sporadic appearances over the years.

Monsieur Roux sold the house with all its contents. He virtually passed stewardship of his parents' past over to me. I inherited everything, from the trousseau already mentioned, to the old man's carefully-folded handkerchiefs, all the crockery and linen of the house, including a twenty-four-piece dinner service and a twelve-piece dessert service by Faience de Gien with each plate bearing a different scene from the life of Joan of Arc. The bits of bed in the attic fitted together to make an entirely comfortable iron-and-brass bedstead. Shelves in the garage fitted neatly into the beautiful wardrobe on a landing, to make a linen-cupboard; they had obviously been there before, and nobody in this house had ever thrown anything away. I kept some furniture, disposed of other, and lamentably sold for a penny-piece the sewing-machine, which I feared I would find nowhere to place. That had been old mother Roux's life and work, and should have stayed. Nevertheless, I had all her hand-made fabrics, and use them still. And I had her portrait cleaned, reframed, and hung above her wooden bed. The husband had been a wine-merchant, hence this was in origin a *maison de vigneron*, and the extent of his tools and handicrafts demonstrated that, between them, this old couple had not wanted for anything. The old bicycle, which some villagers recall seeing Monsieur Roux *père* use seventy years ago, required only the tyres to be pumped, and I could use it again.

Young Monsieur Roux, the eighty-six year-old vendor, had had a son who went to medical school and became a doctor. His doctoral thesis was still in the house. But he had been killed in a motor-cycle accident, and the thesis lay among picture-postcards from before the First War, discarded and uncherished. There was also a daughter, who was married and for whom the fusty house of her grandparents held little interest. When I had refashioned the rooms, I asked Monsieur and Madame to tea, so they could see what I had done; I suppose I also sought their approval. When I told Madame that I was once more using the original Languedocian kitchen, she clapped her hands and exclaimed, 'Oh, ma belle-mère en aurait été contente.'* I did not tell her that I had also found, hidden behind some bricks in the wall, a packet of love-letters written to her husband by a young servant-girl in Montpellier around 1920, in which she promised him everything 'except that', which she begged him not to demand of her. He had obviously forgotten that they had ever existed, still less that he had hidden them from the woman he later married. But they had once mattered, or he would not have kept them. They are now in my library (formerly the attic).

All of which makes one ponder, yet again, the nature of past and future, the purpose of remembrance, the emotional importance of inheritance. I have written elsewhere that, having not met any of my grandparents, and having virtually no idea what sort of people they were, I come without baggage and, being childless, leave without trace. I have therefore been tantalisingly drawn towards families who have a full pregnant

---

* 'My mother-in-law would have been pleased.'

19

past and bursting future, travelling several generations in both directions. Quite apart from his generous character, Andrew Devonshire endeared himself to me, whether he liked it or not, by virtue of being the eleventh duke in an unbroken series, surrounded by the purchases and objects which provided the décor to the lives of the ten others, and in a house built by the ancestress several generations before the first of them. Arvind Singh Mewar, the current Maharana of Udaipur in Rajasthan (more correctly the Maharana of Mewar, but the error is common), is seventy-fifth in line from Bappa Rawul, the founder of the lot in 525, but this is not so heavy with resonance for me, because the line may pass through adoption (although the child adopted to be the next Maharana was usually a cousin, and therefore traceable himself to Bappa Rawul), and because the family has hung on to very little since the break-up of the Raj after the Second World War and the abolition of the Princely States.

Arvind is therefore not strictly a prince in legal terms any longer, but the people of Udaipur know better and will not be robbed of fifteen centuries of their past by the stroke of a pen. When I was writing the history of this most eminent ruling family in India (owing to the fact that they were the only family not to make accommodation with the Moghul invaders when all the other Rajput princes were offering their daughters in order to be granted a quiet life with their jewels, their servants, and their habit of grovelling obeisance, in consequence of which the others are termed 'Maharajah', and only the Mewar prince bears the designation 'Maharana'), I stayed at the palace in Udaipur, or rather at one of them. I travelled every Monday with Arvind to the Temple of Eklingji, some twenty miles distant, where he, as senior servant of the god Shiva, worshipped on behalf of and in the presence of his people. They had no doubt who and what he was.

Added to which, even if the Maharana has fewer possessions than the Duke of Devonshire, he avers the popular belief that he is descended from the Sun. Andrew had to be content with descent from Bess of Hardwick, a less overwhelming light.

When Arvind was on a visit to England some years later, I took him up to Chatsworth for lunch, at Andrew's invitation of course (probably, however, at my suggestion!). On the way there, the Maharana needed to make sure of his protocol, and asked me how he should address the Duke. When we arrived, Andrew drew me quietly into a corner and asked how he should address the prince. So, after a flurry of 'Your Graces' and 'Your Highnesses', they settled into a frosty encounter. The descendant of the Sun was distinctly nervous, not to say scared. The occasion was saved at lunch by Debo, herself the last of a whole herd of Mitfords, who did not mind what anyone called anyone else. She charmed Arvind by asking about his majestically cleft Rajput beard, while Andrew channelled all his attention upon the Maharani, Princess Vijayraj (known as 'Bhuti'), which a lifetime of habit made so natural that not even her awkward silences could deflect him from the pleasure of 'chatting up' a lady.

I wish I had his knack. From the earliest days, at school dances, I nearly always turned a fine opportunity to disaster by saying the wrong thing, and fifty years later I am still doing it, though with perhaps slightly more elegance and originality. At school, it was the awful ignorance of adolescence which propelled me into a black hole when I asked a girl whether she came to the dance-hall often, then volunteered the sneering schoolboy rejoinder without the faintest idea of what it meant. The girl, Christine was her name, pranced off in high dudgeon and refused all subsequent requests for a dance. The echo, fifty years later, came at a dinner hosted by John Julius Norwich at which, after generous helpings of splendid wine, I told a dirty joke to the lady on my right; mercifully, I cannot recall who it was. But the clumsiness, the *gaucherie*, the stupidity, all belonged to the same trait of character. A leopard doesn't change his spots; they may even get bigger.

It is all a matter of tact, of testing the atmosphere and judging what it demands of one. Difficult subjects are not to be avoided at all costs, but they should be summoned at the right moment rather than the wrong one. When I was writing my biography of Georgiana, Duchess of Devonshire, and wondered how to deal with the famous trio of Georgiana, her husband, and her husband's mistress Bess, who was also her closest friend, I felt I had to find some oblique way of collapsing the modern idea that the two women must have had some sexual relations together, simply because in the modern world they do sometimes; it was important, I thought, to see the situation with eighteenth-century eyes. Debo, the present Dowager Duchess, quite bluntly asked whether I thought that all three of them had been to bed at the same time. It was a valid topic because it was relevant, and I was able to reply that one would never know, of course, because crucial passages in their letters had been blacked out by Bess in a determined (and successful) attempt to deny posterity its curiosity. I would not be surprised, however, if Bess had not given Georgiana some tips on how to make herself more alluring to the Duke; hence her references in letters to Georgiana's first-born being as much 'her' child as her mother's. This conversation was plainly chasms away from my appalling attempts to be amusing about delicate matters when heaviness and profundity are what is called for. Sometimes my antennae still let me down.

I have been saved by gracious friends who affect not to notice, and leave me to ruminate, to stew by myself in solitude later, and learn my lessons without the necessity for chastisement. One such was Peggy Wakehurst, whom I visited regularly for about twenty years, until her mind became so fractured and fragile that she didn't know who I was or how – even whether – she knew me. She and her sister Kay Elliott lived into their nineties, and they together illustrated yet again my undilutable fascination with the past, with inheritance of personality and continuation of line. Peggy once told me that her father had been born a hundred and seventy-five years ago, and since the conversation took place in the 1970s, it meant that Dad was alive before the Battle of Waterloo. This startling fact was due to his extraordinary fecundity. He was Charles Tennant, the Glasgow industrialist whose extensive progeny make him the ancestor of, one might guess, a good third of the current aristocracy of England and Scotland; there are Tennants every-where. He had married twice. The first marriage produced ten children, of whom one was Margot Asquith, the Prime Minister's wife. At the age of eighty and a widower, Tennant married for the second time, producing three more daughters – Nancy, Margaret (Peggy) and Katherine (Kay), who all married well and became prominent figures in their different ways. (Kay became briefly famous, when Parliament was first televised, as the peeress who always nodded off when on camera; she had in fact done sterling work long before her drowsiness became a daily feature of life.) This meant that Peggy was able to refer to her 'sister Margot', whom she thought an incorrigible tease, which was an astonishing leap in itself, as Margot Asquith appeared to me to belong to an historical past, not to have a sister taking tea with me. I doubt whether her statement, when she was over ninety, that her father had been born a hundred and seventy-five years before, could possibly be bettered; it must be a record of sorts.

Peggy married Lord Wakehurst, and together they presided as representatives of the monarch, first in Australia after the war, then in Northern Ireland in the 1950s. Through his grandmother, John Wakehurst had inherited the very rickety genes of Elizabeth Gubbins, a mad Irishwoman whose marriage into the family of the Duke of St Albans condemned that unlucky family to generations of imbecility. The strain unfortunately manifested itself, after years of dormancy, in Peggy's second son, whom she cared for well into his adult-hood with exemplary devotion; he was, and still is, a man of strong intelligence, but weak social skills, an affliction akin to autism, which means that he is mostly imprisoned with private thoughts, which he mutters to himself as he paces the room, relentlessly alone amid a whole crowd of family and friends.

Anyway, Peggy was a woman of boundless tact, and a very close friend to me. We could talk of most things, and I did not worry about broaching the subject of her son's condition, about which she was well informed, not just in maternal fashion but substantially, and I know that she welcomed these discussions. She was able to think through the philosophical implications of mental illness, and her own possible responsibility for it having taken a grip on him when he was in his formative years and she was fulfilling duties as vicereine. She did not object to my own reflections on all this, and frequently asked what I thought. There was no tactlessness in alluding to a family unhappiness; on the contrary, it offered a fresh breeze and some mild kind of solace.

But I did forget that Peggy was a woman of her generation, resolutely and unrescuably pre-First World War, for whom some subjects were best left unexamined. On an occasion when I took her to dinner, and she was genuinely perplexed as to why I had not married, especially when there was a young woman to whom I was obviously attached, she pressed me, seeking to be as helpful to me as, perhaps without presumption, I had been to her in talking about her son. Thinking myself sanctioned to be honest, I began to explain the difficulties for any man in proving his affection by the sexual act, as coition could not be faked but was preceded by visible proof of desire. A woman had a much easier time of it. I did not put it quite so crassly, but that was the gist of what I meant, and Peggy knew it.

I had not misjudged the nature and scope of our friendship, but I had cruelly misjudged her ability to give it life in terms of modern discourse. She had neither the shamelessness to talk of such things, nor, more importantly, the vocabulary wherewith to do so. She was lost, adrift, and her rudderless fumbling with words designed to change the subject, when in her heart she wished she could have continued and developed it for my sake, was sad to behold. I had unwittingly played a bad trick on her, and reduced her, in her own eyes, to a witless girl. That was a matter of tact, of antennae, of knowing where to tread and when to divert, and I lacked it.

All of which makes it more than a little astonishing that so many people have felt able to trust me with their secrets, many of which I still keep closeted years after their tellers have forgotten what the secret was about. I suppose it is possible to be both tactless and trustworthy, though not at the same time. Indeed, it is among the lessons that I am still learning, that apparent contradictions are commonplace within every breast and that the man who claims to know anyone with certainty is talking through his hat. It is this very uncertainty about human character which makes all literature possible, even necessary.

I have known a number of people with varying degrees of familiarity, only to realise after their death that I knew nothing whatever about them beyond their congeniality. This is especially true of actors, who devote their art to painful revelation, often tearing themselves to shreds in the process, and devote their lives to obfuscation and concealment. (I speak, of course, of *real* actors, those whose purpose is to portray truth on stage, not the publicity-addicted empty-heads who appear weekly on television and whose pitiable love affairs pack the pages of the Sunday press.) It is as if they actually shrink from being known at all, lest it be discovered that they are not nearly so interesting as the characters they portray. They indeed would make the stuff of literature, because their lives are a massive paradox, professionally bent upon doing the one thing above all that they most fear – showing themselves. Two immediately spring to mind as exemplars: Peggy Ashcroft and Alec Guinness.

It was, oddly enough, Ashcroft who met me, not I who met her. I had written a biography of the nineteenth-century novelist Marie Corelli (disastrously entitled *Now Barabbas was a Rotter*), who reached her apogee in 1895. Her novels were bad, but sold in tens of millions, somewhat like Jeffrey Archer's today, and, also like Archer, she took herself so seriously that she could never understand why she was mocked, ascribing the phenomenon to plain jealousy. She moved from Earl's Court to Stratford-upon-Avon because she thought it right that she should live in the same town as that other great genius of English literature, in order that she could guard his reputation. Her name was false (Minnie Mackay being the honest one), her age was false (claiming to be in her twenties when she was already over fifty, presumably counting on her fans being hopeless at mathematics), she was a liar, a cheat, developed a schoolgirl passion for the painter Arthur Severn which reduced her to baby-talk – the very genesis of Lucia's gabbling in the E. F. Benson series of Mapp and Lucia novels* – and she was terribly, terribly popular. As I have said elsewhere, I was proud of the research undertaken to ferret her out of oblivion, when I had been told at the start that there were no papers available anywhere, but that is another story.

---

* E. F. Benson knew Marie Corelli, and privately mocked her. The Italian infantile gibberish uttered by Lucia is an echo of Corelli.

Shortly after the book appeared, the BBC invited me to adapt it for the wireless. I initially declined, for I knew this was beyond my limited abilities; I was used to thinking in shaped paragraphs, and had no idea how to form dialogue. I thought they should get someone to do the adaptation who was used to working in the genre, and I said so. But the producer insisted, and so I decided that I could not err simply by trying. The only way I could think of tackling the problem was to compromise, to tell the story at one remove, with a narrator, and to have the only character in the text as Marie Corelli herself. I duly finished my version and sent it off, then forgot it. Some six months later the BBC telephoned to say that Peggy Ashcroft had read the script and was eager to play the part of Marie on the radio, if I would agree to be the narrator. More than that, she would be mortified if I said no.

Thus it happened that she and I sat opposite one another at a round table in Broadcasting House, with microphones hovering above us and producers sequestered away in a box somewhere, talking to us through earphones. This is all run-of-the-mill to those who work in the medium, but it was my first experience of the sort, and I was frankly terrified. I need not have worried, for the great Dame Peggy's innate modesty made me feel from the start that I was honouring her, not the other way around, and in rehearsal she sought my approval every time she wanted to give a special intonation to a line. Especially, she asked me whether she could play Marie with a lisp. Now, Marie Corelli did not have a lisp, but I saw straight away that this was a golden piece of actor's intuition – Marie *ought* to have had a lisp, she was the sort of woman who *would* have a lisp. And so she did.

After that, Peggy and I often dined, either at a local restaurant near her home in Hampstead or at the Garrick Club, where she would be my guest. When the club gave her an honorary dinner, it was me they asked to escort her. We went to the theatre together (she was fulsome in her praise of Judi Dench; indeed, who would not be, but I thought it instructive that one great intuitive actress should recognise another at a glance. It is this uncharted and undocumented legacy which actors pass down from one generation to another, I believe, so that Shakespeare's actor Burbage would recognise Donald Sinden today, as Mrs Siddons would recognise Judi Dench). And yet in all that time I could not puncture her unexpected reserve. She had been married to another Garrick member some time before, but would not explore that subject beyond mentioning his name. She had children in Canada, but I never discovered how many, or where they were, or what they did. She was the very antithesis of a gossip, and the undercurrent of her remarks suggested that one should not be interested in something which was not interesting. Only her art was of interest, and that might be worth talking about, although still with an obligatory layer of modesty. She was not arch or flirtatious, just genuinely banal; further, she implied that this was precisely what she should be.

Of course, there might also have been a spot of wise caution in her reluctance to spill beans; perhaps I was a journalist, or would be one day. Having said earlier that I was lucky to have people trust me, it is true that Ashcroft never vouchsafed anything that could not have been gathered by ordinary means. On the other hand, I knew that I could have trusted her with any disclosure, and it would have been safe. It would only have turned up, unexpectedly, as part of the portrayal of a character on stage.

Alec Guinness's fortress door was even more firmly bolted. Whereas with Peggy one might ask a question and receive in reply a sweet-natured evasion, one dare not even ask Guinness anything at all. His privacy was absolute, his reticence forbidding. Even now the totality of Guinness's self-protection mystifies me, for it might seem to suggest more that he had nothing to say than that he preferred not to say it, and yet he was a finely intelligent man, whose books of autobiographical reminiscence betray, at the least, an acute ear for the resonance and harmony of language, for the variety and scope of observation. And they prove the paradox in themselves, for though they are splendid, they are ultimately flat. Alec Guinness remains enigmatic even after three hundred pages of so-called self-portrayal, a blank sheet upon which you may write any kind of character or personality that you wish. It was always said that the most popular actor in Britain, whose work was flattered and valued, even cherished, by the whole country, was so anonymous that one could pass him in the street and not know him. This was utterly true. He was faceless, amorphous, quite unlike any of the famously vivid portrayals he gave on film (his work on stage was less well-known, though better). One might sit next to him at the club and not know to whom one was talking, and he would offer no assistance towards identification, either, but on the contrary might abruptly end the conversation once he had been identified. It was as if he had been rumbled and had to scuttle away to hide.

The profession of acting once again plays some role in this elaborate confection. Guinness was such a miniaturist, so careful and meticulous an assembler of telling details, that it was necessary he should start with a page devoid of feature. He had to have a blank canvas on which to sew his tiny stitches and build a beautiful picture. But one is bound to wonder whether his extraordinary ability to wipe himself away before beginning to construct a character on film was imperceptibly, and perhaps unconsciously, carried over into personal non-professional life, or whether he was such a good actor precisely because he had no ready-made character of his own with which to compete. Did he in fact turn his strange emptiness of feature to professional account? And was that the secret that he feared he might disclose if he were more open in conversation?

I knew him again by accident, and not well by any means. One of my lodgers at Caithness Road was a dear lady with the softest voice and the fuzziest hair like candyfloss called Chattie Salaman. Her sister was Merula Salaman, who had married Alec Guinness. Thus Alec was her brother-in-law, though, typically of that clan, Chattie had talked about Alec for months before letting on which Alec she meant. We met for dinner at Italian restaurants sometimes, and I might see him at the club, but nothing of the conversation was ever striking enough to be remembered. Only twice did he gingerly step out of the shell and invite a closer acquaintance, and on both occasions I responded in entirely the wrong way, and the shell clamped tight once more.

Some American friends were in London and had bought tickets for the Alan Bennett play in which Guinness was playing the lead. I was invited to accompany them, and it happened that I was with him at dinner in an Italian restaurant the week before, and found reason to announce the impending visit. 'You will come round back-stage afterwards, won't you?' he asked, in that ever-diffident voice, a remark which I construed as an invitation. In the event, when I did go back-stage with three guests in attendance, Guinness affected to be surprised and irritated, greeted us perfunctorily in the corridor and dismissed us within seconds. I afterwards heard that I had been roundly chastised by him. 'You see what you get,' he said, 'when you allow anyone to get close? That young man has taken advantage of his connection with my sister-in-law, I might have known he would.'

Later, I was staying the weekend with a girl-friend near Hindhead, which was only a few miles away from the Guinnesses' home on the road to Portsmouth. I think Chattie was staying with them that same weekend, which would account for his having known where I was. Anyway, the telephone unaccountably rang at Debbie's farmhouse, with a message for me. When I answered, there was the quiet, polite voice of Alec Guinness. 'Merula and I thought you might like to come here for a spot of lunch,' he said. I hastily thought how nice that would be, but I was, after all, somebody else's guest, and it would have been unthinkable, to me at least, to chuck one host in order to indulge another. I explained the circumstances, and hoped I might visit another time. That was the second brick. It had obviously taken such effort on his part to break the habit of tense withdrawal, actually to invite intrusion, that my refusal to acknowledge the gesture was tantamount to a denigration of it. Did I not realise what it had taken for him to pick up the phone? Did I place so little value on his invitation?

That, of course, is unfair. I was not asked again, but I seriously doubt if self-importance had anything to do with it. Guinness was the least vainglorious of men, and I suspect his shyness might have made him relieved that I had turned him down, and that, having tried once, he need never try again. Another little anecdote confirms the point. When I was in Milwaukee working on the Jeffrey Dahmer trial, Dahmer's lawyer professed an admiration for Guinness and asked whether I might be able to get his autograph. I wrote and asked Alec, who immediately obliged, but with the added typical footnote, 'I can't think why such a small thing should matter.'

To finish with a trio of actors all adept at concealment, but in hugely different ways, I need to consider the case of Donald Sinden. If Ashcroft smilingly deflected, and Guinness drew up the bridge with a clang, Sinden made it impossible to find out anything about him simply by talking all the time and regaling his interlocutor with such a torrent of amusing stories that intimate conversation was banished as irrelevant. All three of these people were brilliant, at times electrifying, on stage, and all three were undiscoverable in person. Donald I knew best of the three, for he was a Trustee of the Garrick Club as well as one of its most frequent visitors. Besides, his wife Diana and I were occasional colleagues in so far as we both gave lunch lectures to assemblies of bored country ladies as part of our living. I never met a more outwardly friendly or garrulous man, gregarious to a degree, always surrounded, loudly entertaining all and sundry, charming to strangers, disarming to ladies, and theatrical to the fingernail. His voice, rounded like the Elizabethan stage on which it was designed to be heard, echoing and reverberating in all four corners of the room, his eyebrows lifted to illustrate a point (one imagined the dark make-up brush on them to enable them to be seen at the back of the stalls), eyes and sonorities penetrating the space around, it was impossible not to be aware of Donald's presence and congeniality. He was the best anecdotalist I ever encountered, with hundreds of stories, all true (or very nearly so), and new ones added weekly to the store. If anything funny or bizarre was due to happen, one would be certain that Donald would be there to register it. Alas, none of these stories retain their dazzle and delivery in print, and so one must hope somebody will have the savvy to place a recording-machine in front of Donald for five hours and get them all down for posterity. Let it only be said, that he was enormous fun.

And yet there was an embarrassment about Sinden which flustered him whenever something more enduring and valuable than a funny story threatened to pop up. He could not handle friendship which was expressed in any other way than through banter, the slightest hint of emotion turning him to stuttering stone. And this was a man whose stage perform-ances (*King Lear* especially springs to mind) were torrential in their emotional sweep and depth of charge. The emotional potential was there in abundance, but he was terrified lest it should show in the real world. Perhaps he knew its power all too well, and feared what he might become if his emotional self were unleashed; to judge by his performances, he had good cause to worry.

Donald suffered an acute bereavement, which is mercifully visited upon few men. His son Jeremy, like him an actor, with several portrayals in television costume drama to his credit, died in his early forties of cancer, leaving wife and young children to mourn him. And Donald mourned as only a father whose son predeceases him can mourn, with presumably bitterness at fate and some justifiable rancour, but none of this ever showed. It was difficult even to commiserate, because he did not welcome any kind of emotional bonding which an expression of sorrow must needs promote, and one saw immediately that it was far better to let him nurse his bereavement alone, and continue to be jolly and ebullient with us. It was out of respect for his privacy, no doubt, but it was also due to anxiety that he would not know what to do if one were to offer tactile condolence and that it would be deeply unfair to subject him to that kind of test.

Then, once when I was staying with Donald and Diana at their country retreat in Kent (I was researching at Ellen Terry's house near by, and needed Donald for all the history and anecdote about Terry which neither the house nor the papers could offer), and no mention of Jeremy had been made, he suddenly asked me to accompany him to the top of a hill, on the property, with a distant view in all directions. 'It was Jeremy's favourite spot,' he said, then, hesitant as ever, lest he had allowed too much to slip even by so undramatic a remark, 'if you're sure you don't mind?' We walked up the gentle slope, and then surveyed the scene which Jeremy had so appreciated. Donald said the family thought it best to remember him with a tree planted on the spot, better than a grey gravestone. That was all. No intimate revelation. No breakdown. But a moment of remarkable companionship for a man so taut and corseted. 'It was good of you to come,' he said. No more eloquent, or emotional, statement could be imagined.

I have strayed somewhat from the ghosts of this house in Castries, their past images plastered on the walls for future gawpers, through my own interest in the past, having none by inheritance; *faux pas*; the delicacies of conversation and the vulnerabilities of professionally extrovert people, but I suspect they are all connected, for they are diverse manifestations of my own clumsy attempts to be part of a whole, to fit in as an essential element of a long and complex jigsaw puzzle. We none of us want to feel contingent, unnecessary, what Jean-Paul Sartre called *de trop*, a feeling of drifting dispensability, which made him feel physically sick and which he described with disgust as 'viscosity'. It was this notion of 'not mattering' because we were mere cogs in a celestial machine which gave rise to his fierce philosophy of existentialist wrath (or at least his version of it). To a much less noisy degree we must all feel something of this anxiety, for the unspoken truth is that we do not matter, and that every way in which we can disguise this awful realisation, whether through philosophy – turning circular thought into an art – or through religion, or through genetic inheritance in families, is to be embraced with clutching relief. The pitfalls of conversation remind one constantly of the transitoriness of all effort, that it will all sink into insignificance in the end, and the self-protection of the shy is a sublime attempt to prevent the problem of human unimportance from ever having to be faced. Great actors who are also shy are lucky in being able to face the problem by proxy, through somebody else's words and in somebody else's skin, and immediately afterwards retreat into their shrugging non-involvement. I have never met an actor who will talk philosophy, or knows how to; he acts it instead.

There was a particular moment, not so long ago, when I attempted to invent my own future by stratagem. I did not realise at the time what was really going on in my head, but now it seems clear. It related to my old school, Wilson's Grammar, founded in 1615 and resident in Camberwell from that day until long after I left in 1958. The school had been crucial in my metamorphosis from Old Kent Road layabout to promising young man; it had shown me the glories and secrets of literature, the virtues of responsibility, the craft of language, and so much else, especially perhaps the release from having to apologise for myself all the time. I owed the school a great deal, at times I imagined almost everything, and I longed for some way in which to demonstrate my debt and my recognition of it. The first thing I did, about thirty years after I left, was to buy new gowns for the school prefects. They were a rich blue, like the black gowns of the teachers but bordered in blue velvet, and the five prefects had the right to wear them in return for the huge responsibilities for discipline which fell upon them. In the years that had passed, all those responsibilities had been abandoned (imagine the outcry now if a seventeen-year-old had the duty of punishing a fifteen-year-old with six strokes of the cane on his backside), but the gowns remained as a symbol of maturity, I suppose. They had grown threadbare; when I visited the school for the first time in thirty years, I recognised the same old gown that I had myself worn. Seeing the tattered label of Ede and Ravenscroft, I was able to visit that ancient establishment in Chancery Lane and commission some new gowns at my expense. I had them delivered to the school, and heard nothing more. No letter of thanks, no word of wonderment, only silence. I might as well have thrown them into the Thames.

That I put down to bad manners, that the headmaster of a

school for boys had yet himself to learn the simple arts of social behaviour. I thought nothing more of it. Meanwhile, headmasters changed, and a new young man, about thirty-two, took over. His name, absurdly (though not for him I'm sure), was Chris Tarrant. I invited him to dine at the Garrick Club, where it was evident that he enjoyed himself, and indeed he was fresh and pleasant company. Suddenly, without preamble or precognition, the idea struck me. Why could not I start a new Wilson's Grammar tradition, namely an annual dinner at the Garrick Club for the school prefects of that year? I would take the large table for eight opposite the door in the Coffee Room (the hugely elegant main dining-room of the club, dripping with glorious paintings and boasting the most refined and harmonious proportions of any room in London, a fact in itself guaranteed to promote contentment), from which the boys would have a perfect view as well as being made to feel part of a really special event. There would be the five prefects, the headmaster and his wife, and myself. It would become part of the school calendar, say in the third week of September, and I would hope that the tradition would quickly establish itself as something the sixth-form looked forward to every year. I was quite certain that none of them could ever have engineered a like occasion for themselves, and probably nearly all of them would not even have been north of the river to the West End in their lives. It was proper that an older man should be able to offer such a treat to delight and inform the young, for the annual Garrick dinner would, in its small but enduring way, be part of their education. I would guarantee to be responsible for the event, and pay for it all, every year for the rest of my life.

I was greatly enthusiastic about the plan even as I imagined it, out loud, in conversation with Mr Tarrant. It would be my method of giving something back to the school, and a better one I could not conceive. Tarrant said nothing definitive, but appeared to take on some of my enthusiasm. I said I would write formally to make the proposition.

His reply to my letter was one of the most staggering blows I ever received. He said that, on reflection, and in view of the fact that I was unmarried and had frankly hinted at the causes of my bachelorhood, he thought it better, given the current climate, 'in this day and age', that he should decline my proposal. What he was suggesting was that five seventeen- or eighteen-year-old boys, in the company of their headmaster and his wife, were not safe to dine with a single man in a room packed with sixty other persons, and in a gentleman's club of the utmost respectability. I was a threat to their moral well-being even as they were eating their Beef Wellington. Of course the idea was absurd, but I could not bring myself to laugh. I was appalled by Tarrant's cowardice in turning down something of value in order to earn marks from the Politically Correct Brigade. And I was personally insulted. My gift was besmirched by his pusillanimity. I was well and truly shat upon. 'I hope you are not offended,' he wrote.

'You bet I'm bloody offended,' I replied. The rest of my letter was not splenetic, but certainly angry. I said that I would have nothing whatever to do with the school in the future, and I have never done so. Not that I imagine this little threat matters to them, or to Tarrant himself. But the damage to myself was far greater even than the refusal of generosity. I now see that the annual Garrick Prefects' Dinner would have been my progeny of a sort, my continuity, my escape from the viscosity of a hapless markless existence. I would not have needed gratitude; the event itself would have brought a smile to my face.

Instead of which I have these brownish old photographs of somebody else's ancestors on the walls of my guest-room, giving them, in death, a relevance which they could not have anticipated. And I still look for my own relevance to the future.

37

CHAPTER TWO

The Skin of My Teeth

Peggy Münster first asked me to escort her to Ireland in about 1972. The Countess Münster, widow of a German *Graf* and a member of the ubiquitous Ward family, lived alone in a splendid cosy spacious house in Oxfordshire – Bampton Manor, surrounded by one of the finest gardens in England, which was frequently featured in magazine articles. Her days of riot had been in the 1920s, and now she was a frail, thin, wrinkled old lady, still with fire in her eyes, a strong manly voice and the vanity to dress well and look good. The vestiges of great beauty were discernible in her fine face, and of great spirit in her frank enjoyment of company and laughter. A cook and a housekeeper looked after her, but she would get out of the house and visit every day if she were invited. She drove herself, taking the middle of the road as being the safest bet if you could not remember whether you should be on the left or the right, and at a speed fit to win rallies; I was often scared when Peggy was at the wheel. Down the road at Pusey, another big house with a giant garden and grounds, lived 'Sister Nic', mother of Simon Hornby of the W. H. Smith business, and a little farther was Robert Heber-Percy, still living at Lord Berners' exotic and daft house at Faringdon, with its tame doves flying around, each dyed a different colour. In the other direction was Hardy Amies in a converted schoolroom. I looked forward to weekends at Bampton because Peggy always managed to produce some character out of a history book to have lunch with. And then she asked me to accompany her for a week or two in Ireland, as guests of an eccentric and hugely wealthy American art-collector called Henry McIlhenny.

Henry's only demands were that his guests should talk and that they should bring their dinner-jackets. If they failed in either respect they would be given a tray in their bedroom and never invited again. Otherwise staying with him was a dream-like experience, as if one had suddenly discovered one had a rich, benevolent, kindly uncle who waved wands and created magic. His house, Glenveagh Castle in County Donegal, was romantic beyond all likelihood, and the life within it like an amalgam of *Brideshead Revisited* and *Le Grand Meaulnes*, warm in comfort, luxurious in taste. Henry had bought the castle (and the lake and the mountains all around) just before the Second World War, and spent five months a year there from May to September, stopping off at the Connaught Hotel in London on the way, and tempering the assault on his senses with con-valescence at an Italian spa before returning to the United States. His main home was half a square in the centre of Phila-delphia, and most of his personal art collection hung on per-manent loan in the Philadelphia Museum; the rest was on his own walls in Rittenhouse Square or at Glenveagh Castle.

Henry would send a car and scrumptious sandwiches to Belfast airport to meet his guests and transport them through a green but dreary landscape to the distant wonder of Donegal. As one drove up into the mountains tinted with heather and shadow one knew one was about to enter Wonderland, and the vista which opened beyond the gates to the estate never failed to excite. One leant forward to see it all, darting eyes from left to right in order to miss nothing. The drive, two or three miles long, was loaded with rhododendrons, and when they stopped, down on the right was the magnificent calm lake, stretching into the distance, with high hills to frame it and the cool majesty of Nature's silence. If you were lucky you might catch sight of a lone stag surveying the world from a peak, its antlers silhouetted against the sky, a painter's model. The drive turned round the brow of a hill and there was Glenveagh itself, perched all alone on a promontory, tall and proud with towers piercing the sky and its very own scenery as backdrop. You caught your breath at the sight.

To the side and behind the castle were extensive gardens, laid out by Henry himself and designed both to walk through and admire, and to provide cut flowers, enough to fill twenty fresh vases every day. There was a special room set aside for this, and if one could not find Henry it was a fair guess he would be in the garden room cutting flowers or in the kitchen checking ingredients. It sounds an exaggeration even to me as I write this, but the food in this remote corner of Donegal, prepared by a local Irishwoman from Letterkenny on instructions from Henry, and destined to be eaten only by people in the house, was the finest I have eaten anywhere in the world, not excepting the famous restaurant tables of Paris and Lyon.

The attention to detail at Glenveagh Castle was fastidious, even fussy and feminine, but immensely charming. Each bedroom was decorated in a different colour-scheme, carefully blending tints and hues of carpet, wallpaper, curtains, ornaments, desk furnishings, letter-opener and cushions. If you were in the yellow room, a vase of specially selected yellow flowers would be brought in every morning after breakfast, while the blue room was given shades of blue flowers and the red room varieties of red, russet and bronze. Breakfast was always brought to you in bed. This was obligatory, as nobody was allowed in the dining-room before lunch and there was no breakfast-room. It came on a tray laden with scarcely believable bone china, a yellow set for the yellow room, tints of red and pink for the red room, delicate blues for the blue bedroom, and so on. The salt and pepper pots were likewise co-ordinated, as were the napkins, and the one flower on the side of the tray. It was a cause of some frustration to somebody somewhere that scrambled eggs turned out in one colour only.

There must have been over twenty sets of this breakfast china, and heaven knows how many dinner services as well, for we never dined off the same plates twice. For five months there were never fewer than fourteen for lunch (being Henry and all the house-guests) and twenty for dinner (including people who motored from afar for the meal). Henry entertained in lavish style, but scrupulously without pretension. The food was perfect, not ostentatious; the plates were fine, because Henry liked beautiful things; we dressed for dinner, because it turned a meal into a pleasant occasion; servants brought the dishes in, because this ensured that everybody was served while the food was hot; conversation was free and cheerful, because Henry liked to enjoy himself and liked even more to be the cause of enjoyment in others.

He sat at the head of the table with his back to a roaring peat fire which was lit even in high summer. We might feel the room was marginally too stuffy, but Henry would dine in his overcoat with a scarf if he felt chilly, which he was likely to in all weathers. He led the conversation with ease, never allowing pause or awkwardness to descend, for he had a fund of stories, much experience of the world, and always invited interesting people who could share and respond. His voice was full of peaks and valleys, rising and dipping, coloured by a permanent grin and an incipient tease. He loved having something to laugh at, and looked as if he was ever on the point of saying something naughty, but never did. His sense of mischief was child-like and direct, written in twinkling eyes and roguish smile, not subtle and inventive like a practised raconteur, and he preferred table-talk to be amusing rather than impressive. If he had something serious to say, it would be in a private one-to-one encounter, which he might contrive during a walk in the garden, and on matters of art there were few people in the world to gainsay him. Only that youthful exuberant genius David Carritt* knew more than he did, and Henry was quick to acknowledge the fact. Carritt was a regular guest.

Henry McIlhenny was one of the princes of this world, a man one was bound to love, and at whose passing one was honoured to grieve. He illustrated one of the secrets of a happy life, too often despised by the rich: that money is useless unless it gives pleasure. His money gave pleasure to those privileged to be his friends as well as those lucky to work for him, and his generosity was boundless. His art collection in America was bequeathed to the museum. Glenveagh Castle, contents and estate he left to the Irish nation, and it is now open to the public. I was among the last people to be within its walls when it was private, alive with laughter and the joyful ease of good company.

Shamefully, he was quickly forgotten, as if he had served his purpose and need not engage our attentions further. A simple memorial service was held at a village church in Ireland. It was attended by his servants, his cook, his Irish friends, and of all the hundreds of English guests who had enjoyed his hospitality repetitively over many years, only two of us made the journey from London to be present. When Ross Hamilton, the Pimlico antique dealer, attempted to organise a similar service in London, he was discouraged by severe lack of interest. Today Henry's name is remembered in art-history circles, and perhaps observed by Bloody Mary drinkers on the bottles of Tabasco sauce, the recipe for which (it was said) his family owned, and from whence his wealth derived, but it has otherwise evaporated. He had no children, and his sister died in the same

---

* David Carritt (1927–1982), art-historian and dealer.

year as he. One of the great characters of the twentieth century is thus blown from the record like a camel-print in the desert.

Is it any wonder that I revert time and time again to the remorselessness of the unproductive fate? Henry produced much in mirth and congeniality, he was a prime exemplar of the grace of social intercourse, and his knowledge of fine art was widely recognised and valued. Yet he is now a name at the Philadelphia Museum and in the odd footnote in learned tomes. Progeny are not merely a source of pride (and, one might add, of anxiety), but a guarantor of future significance. Generations may pass, but one's signature continues to reside, slightly diluted with each new coupling, in the demeanour, behaviour or talents of the descendants. An alternative is for one's personality to be labelled and conserved for all time in one's work, as with an artist, a novelist, a composer, a scientist with original insight, or a contributor to philosophic theory. A childless art-collector does not stand a chance.

In that sense, Michelangelo and Dickens, Zola and Mozart live not just as names, but as people. The man would be impervious indeed who spent time with the statues and paintings of Michelangelo, or read his sonnets, and did not feel that he *knew* the young Buonarotti, bursting with enthusiasm for human form, singing with lyrical appreciation of muscular beauty and the harmony of a shape produced by centuries of subtle (and to him, purposeful) evolution, wracked with anguish at his inability finally to express the spiritual basis of this love with anything but a tentative approximation, growing gradually into loneliness and frustration. It is all there. So is he, today. He speaks to us still. And Mozart is a living presence of joy, serenity, despair, disillusion, and triumphant soaring vision to whoever has ears to listen and a heart to receive. (It is frankly incomprehensible to me that throughout the first half of the twentieth century Mozart's music was disregarded and underprized, the majority of symphonies and sonatas never heard and never played, as if his voice were muffled by philistine prison-guards. With Edwin Fischer and Clara Haskill this unbelievable neglect was rectified, but the full rediscovery of Mozart's genius did not really flourish until my early youth. Can genius really be passed over by fashion? It would seem so.)

The tortured, dark soul of Emily Brontë is brought to us with a handful of poems and one novel, as clear and crystalline now as ever they were. Even the incorrigibly slippery Shakespeare, about whom we are supposed to know nothing, and whose plays are supposed to reveal nothing personal, can be summoned into real life with concentration. The sonnets alone reveal a man of grave subtlety and intensity of emotion, painfully alive to the fragility of time and fame and temper. His portrait of King Richard III is, I am fond of saying (and in this I know of what I speak), the first psychologically convincing account of a serial killer's mind and method, which testifies to the author's penetrating understanding of the human soul. Gertrude is the finest portrayal of the bewilderment and sexual ambivalence of motherhood, Hamlet himself a searing display of primeval anguish and doubt. One could go on for pages (and many have gone on for whole books on the subject), but suffice it to say that Shakespeare is not dead. He is there in his words and in the subjects of his searching enquiry; he speaks to us still. All attempts to pretend that he is a superb craftsman whose constructs reveal nothing personal are foolish. You would need to be as receptive as a mollusc to believe that.

Actors are a different species. It is said that one has to be witness to a performance on stage to know the effect of an actor's performance, that their art dies with them. As I have said elsewhere, I challenge this, too. I have seen Olivier and Gielgud on stage, and the great French actress Edwige Feuillère, and the consummate Spanish actress Nuria Espert, and I live even now with the effect of their performances on me at the time. But I also know the art of Edmund Kean and Charles Mathews and Charles Macready, for I have seen them passed down through generations of other performers to be given fresh life today with actors performing now; not imitators, but inheritors. That is progeny of a rare kind, defying genetics altogether, like the kidnapping of a soul. I believe this is what actors do anyway, every time they go on stage. To do it to one another, by a kind of generational osmosis, is but an extension of their uncommon genius.

With the recording in sound and on celluloid that is available today, one might imagine that past actors can be *immediately* available to present audiences. This is not necessarily true. You have a better idea of Olivier's impact through a contemporary actor inheriting his style and presence, and thereby having a direct dialogue with you, than you would through the medium of film, which reduces Olivier to mannerism and technique. The very fact of inscribing *one* performance *one* day on to history and regarding it as definitive, or even approximating to the energy of a live performance, is slightly necrophiliac. It is more alert to the deadness of a recorded image than to the vibrancy of the real thing. The record can only repeat itself; an actor never does.

There are some actors, of a more pedestrian level perhaps, whose performances are preserved by modern technology, and for this we must be thankful. Still I wonder whether these recordings are a true legacy – a kind of inheritance if you like – or a rather brutal nail in the coffin, hammered in with renewed vigour on each showing.

I knew Richard Beckinsale very well when we were both in our twenties. He and his girlfriend Judy Loe were among the new crop of friends I made at the repertory company in Crewe, in the days when young actors learned their trade through hard slog, rehearsing one play while playing another, their minds stocked with several roles at once. (A generation earlier, it was even common for actors to have to carry the whole of the classical canon in their heads, Sir Donald Wolfit famously being able to play Hamlet, Macbeth, Lear, Richard III or Othello at the drop of a hat, and perhaps playing two or three of them in one week.) The *alumni* of 1966 included Trevor Jones, Brendan Price, Gwen Taylor, Valerie Phillips (all of whom moved in to live with me at Caithness Road), Maggie Ollerenshaw, Richard Beckinsale and Judy Loe. Judy was one of the most beautiful women imaginable, with large, lively eyes, a broad smile revealing teeth so perfect they might have been designed by an advertiser, matchless complexion, and luscious black hair forming naturally into generous waves. Her real name was Judy St Loe, and I implored her to retain her sainthood, as I suspected such an unusual name would do no harm in a profession as reliant upon luck and whimsy as on talent, but she would not budge, and has done quite well enough without it. Also, she caught from somewhere that indescribable theatrical manner, a fusion of exaggeration and exuberance, which is sometimes called 'camp'; Judy did not whisper, she was not tentative, she burst into a room like a firework, face and eyes aglow, laughter at the ready. No wonder Richard fell for her.

He, in contrast, was a most unlikely actor. Quiet, understated, modest, thoroughly enjoying the company of his more extrovert friends in 'the business' but never tempted to compete with them, he gave the impression of somebody who might have been a footballer, or a disc jockey, or even a chatty local butcher, but who had somehow been pushed into acting at somebody else's suggestion. I have no idea if this was true or not, but Richard certainly did not seem to bear the burning mark of somebody who is 'driven', as so many actors are, to go on stage not through choice but by exigent necessity. He was the most gloriously easy company, good-natured and fun, the source and provocation of merriment in others rather than a fountain of wit in himself. Everybody wanted to please him, to make him happy, to give him a pleasant evening. And everybody wanted his career to prosper; there never was a more popular man in the profession.

Richard did not take himself too seriously. He was not earnest or obsessive, but he quietly made a mark which was unique. He looked very agreeable, by which I mean that he did not boast what used to be called 'matinée idol' good looks of classical dimensions, because he did not need to. Rather was his especial handsomeness derived from the play on his features of his innate goodness of character, decency and modesty combined to make him appear everybody's 'mate', the bloke on the corner who would not let you down and who was always good for a lark. And, in the fashion of the day, his hair was long to his shoulders and copious.

He and Judy were married (his second marriage, itself unexpected in one so young) and were delightfully happy together, in a way which was intoxicating to behold, without for one moment descending into touchy-demonstrations which might cloy or be embarrassing to others. They soon had a daughter, Kate, who is now herself an international film-star of limpid beauty. Kate was still a little girl, maybe about five, when it was discovered that Judy's fallopian tubes were blocked and that it would be unlikely that she could conceive a second time. As she and Richard both wanted their family to grow, they took advice and were told there was a good chance that an operation might do the trick and put Judy's body back into baby-bearing shape. They agreed to take that chance, and she duly was admitted to hospital.

The operation was declared a total success, but by the grimmest collision of circumstances, which even the dramatists of Ancient Greece, themselves masters of the cool art of vicious irony, might not have dared to invent, the doctors were unable to give Judy the news unalloyed. They had also to announce to her that her husband Richard had died in the night, victim of a heart-attack at the age of thirty-one. Kate says that her father had had a premonition of his imminent passing, and that she had felt the wind of calamity brush through the house that night.

The tragedy for Judy was of cruel dimensions. But what did Richard's death mean for his public, for his fans and admirers, for those millions who watched him regularly on television? It meant, of course, sadness and a shiver of fear that fate could fall so undeservedly. But these things pass easily, and it is perhaps safer that they should; we cannot spend every day con- templating the vicissitudes of life – that was Hamlet's trouble. But in the case of Richard Beckinsale something less fathom- able, perhaps even more sinister, was at work. The public did not lament him too long, because they still had him, frozen and congealed in scores of recorded performances. With the advances of video machines, they could turn him on, bring him to life as it were, whenever the mood took them. He was *theirs* in a way which was fundamentally different from the way in which he was Judy's. Her bereavement would never be fully assuaged, even though her life continued and evolved happily; *their* loss was repaired at the push of a button.

It should be recalled that at the time of his death Richard was already a 'star' of at least two television series, *Porridge* and *Rising Damp*. His easy charm was as if made for television, his technique so invisible that it appeared he was not acting at all, but simply 'behaving' in a natural manner. It is this kind of natural acting, massively removed from the pyrotechnical wizardries of a Wolfit or a Sinden, that has always been mis- understood by the public and mistakenly relegated to the second-eleven team. It was the style of work which made Gerald du Maurier appear on stage as if he had walked in off the street and had no idea an audience was watching him. It showed also in the studied nonchalance of Allan Aynesworth, who used the stage as his drawing-room. Richard had it to a superlative degree, and the pity is that he did not live long enough for his art to have been developed and matured on stage. But the consequence of this style, when produced on television in the corner of the room opposite the sofa, is that the actor appears to be precisely that – a *product* – to be consumed by the public to a surfeit if they so wish, without their involvement in the art, or their reception of the magic. And so, does Richard have a kind of immortality in these archive recordings, still watched today by people who were not born when he died? Or are they in a weird way a kind of insult to him, akin to sticking a pin through a butterfly and placing it in a glass case? The beauty of the butterfly has gone with the movement of its wings, only the satisfaction of the collector remains. So, too, the gaiety and immediacy of Richard, whether as friend or as actor, cannot be served by disinterring him weekly for the delectation of an undiscerning public. That is what I mean by 'necrophiliac'; it is unhealthy. His legacy for us lies in the work of other actors today, just as his was inherited from the likes of du Maurier and Aynesworth. His legacy for Judy is in the character and talent of Kate Beckinsale. Thus does he have a dual future, public and private; whereas the archives of his TV shows are collectors' glass cases – the very antithesis of a future.

I can hear the objections now, that there are many actors whose magic is recreated with each celluloid rerun, not re-buried with every peep-hole viewing of the deceased. I myself think immediately of one majestic exception, the astonishingly alive Marilyn Monroe. One cannot watch *Some Like It Hot* or *The*

Misfits without registering the glowing vividness of her personality, her piercing vulnerability and extravagant, almost impossible, *naïveté*. She seems to have cheated death, to step forward triumphantly from oblivion with defiant, if rather nervous, panache. It is hard to think of any others; Greta Garbo, Charlie Chaplin, Fredric March, are all set in ice, to be watched as museum exhibits might be examined and admired. They have become *things*, petrified representatives of their time. Their recorded performances are that – mere records – lacking the red corpuscle and the vibrancy of life. I imagine they themselves would have preferred these records not to be shown; instead, they would have wanted their artistry to be inherited by other actors, carrying their torch forward for them and causing it to burn anew. I would not mind betting that this would also have been the attitude of Richard Beckinsale. So why is Marilyn so different? Why does she break the rule?

Somebody I know who worked with her said she was not an actress at all, that she simply couldn't do it. Although I disagreed fundamentally with him at the time, for the very reason that her performances were still watchable, I now think he hit the nail on the head. It is because Marilyn Monroe was no actress, that she had no legacy of art to bequeath, that any such legacy is not traduced by resurrecting her at every opportunity. She dominated the screen for who she was, not for who she was trying unsuccessfully to be, and she still reaches out as a fragile human being talking directly to the audience, through the words, behind the words, in spite of the words she is given to say. Forget the acting; this is a person you can grasp and find utterly palpable. Her husband Arthur Miller saw this more than all the directors and actors who tried to work with her and gave up in frustrated despair, which is why he wrote *The Misfits* for her. That film looked to be her testament, but it has turned out to be her survival. With it, and *Some Like It Hot* (even the otherwise execrable *How to Marry a Millionaire*), Marilyn is the odd one out, the one who does not die, who has cheated fate. Because she was the odd one out long before she died.

Talking of death (and I am reluctant to advance it as a subject, for I really intend this to be a book about life and renewal and continuance, but let's see how it goes), I have myself been at least three times within inches of finality. Anyone who has moved that close to his end, almost before his beginning has really got under way, will confirm that the experience forces one to become a philosopher, to think, as it were, for the first time ever, really to ponder and ruminate upon the fickleness of providence. It is the king of all clichés to say that every day starts to count thereafter, but the point of clichés is to be universally true. In my case, it may go some way towards explaining why I have so often written about people who bring down this curtain in so vicious, sudden, cruel and premature a fashion. They people every page of *The Evil That Men Do*, and yet the book itself throbs with the goodness which graces many lives. It is an attempt to put in one's marker for human character while one still can.

My parents moved from the smothering smog of London to South Wales when I was sixteen years old, as it became imperative for my mother's health that she escape an air which was slowly choking her. They accepted, in exchange for their prefab in Camberwell, a tiny terraced house in Barry, and there the fresh sea air blasted through the front door every time one went to fetch the milk from the doorstep. I remained behind in London, but went to visit from time to time, hitch-hiking all the way; there was no M4 and no Severn Bridge, so one went in stages from London to Oxford to Gloucester to Chepstow to Cardiff. Even without stopping, the direct route would take any driver six hours. Once, I took my old school-friend Bernard Fane with me. It was meant to be an enormous treat, for we London boys never got anywhere near the sea and never saw a field, but grew up entirely surrounded by buildings, stunting our spirit.

Down on the coast were some steep and beautiful cliffs at a spot called The Knap, green on top but descending down to clusters of great rocks at their foot, against which the waves beat and crashed and sprayed at high tide. Beyond the rocks was gentle sand, and at low tide the waves receded so far into the distance that their ferocity could no longer be heard and therefore, by London boys, could not be suspected. We knew absolutely nothing of nature and its laws. We believed only what we saw, and we saw calm.

We also saw that it was a short climb to the top of the cliff, perhaps thirty feet, and there were short trees on its face, jutting out at right angles, ready to be grabbed and held. We had never climbed anything before in our lives, and we determined (I think, to my horror, that it was my idea) that we should climb this cliff before going home to tea. There was nobody about, for it was not strictly the holiday season; in any case, sea-lovers did not go to The Knap to lie down, as I subsequently found out.

I went first, Bernie following on below and behind me. The first surprise was that the cliff was very much higher than my eyes had judged, but I suppose I soon reached a point where I did not want to back down and shame myself. It was going to take longer than I had anticipated. So what? Bernie, more sensible than I, recognised the difficulty after barely ten feet, and withdrew. I went on, up and up, until I reached a point where to retreat was becoming dangerous. To my intense surprise, the face of the cliff was becoming ever more gritty and crumbly as I went higher, and, worse still, its gentle slope, which had alone made the climb a feasible endeavour, surrendered to a totally vertical face. I clung on to the sparse bits of vegetation which I had seen from below, and they, too, were becoming sparser the higher I went. With very little to grab hold of, and cascades of debris falling below me with every movement of my foot, I very quickly realised I was in trouble, and real fear gripped my heart.

I flattened myself against the cliff, one foot perched on a small, only slightly firm, ledge, the other dangling, my left arm beneath my chin, my right arm gripping a piece of root, and I was so scared that I dared not move. I could certainly go no higher, and the only way down was to fall. I must by then have been about a hundred feet above the ground, and when I turned my head a mere fraction of an inch to see what was below, I dislodged more dirt which went crashing down, so far below me that I could not hear its landing, and the merciless boulders looked like pebbles. I kept as still as I could. I thought I was going to die.

It is quite true that one's past life rushes before one's eyes in such a situation. There was not much past to speak of, at that time, but I did think of my mother, and how she would suffer when my body was discovered, of all that she had done for me, of my parents' hopes for me and their work towards realising those hopes. I wanted to say I was sorry, that I didn't mean it. At no time did I either wonder what I was missing (that is, regret that the future was going to be cancelled; I had no great plans, and that was hardly a moment to be thinking of them) or imagine that it would hurt when my body hit the rocks. My thoughts were of sorrow for the unhappiness I was going to cause, and regret that I had pushed myself into so stupid a predicament. I went on thinking similar circular thoughts for however long I hung there – perhaps an hour. And I also prayed, violently and ferociously, for myself.

I then heard movement above me. A man was descending on a rope from the distant skies, and I dared to look up without moving my head. He came level with me, and hoisted the rope, which was around him, over my head so that it held us both. I thought even then, this is going to go wrong, he can't do it, the rope will slip, I am better off staying as I am, without moving, like a mussel on the rock who is not bothered by the moving waters about it. The man, fortunately, knew better. Having secured me, he signalled to his colleagues above and we were both hauled up, to what seemed to me like aircraft height, to safety. I was given oxygen, and passed out, I forget in which order.

Bernie had run to find somebody, who had spied me, a tiny unshifting black spot on the cliff face, and had called the Fire Brigade. I was rescued by men in uniform, but they could have been in pantomime costume for all it mattered. I remember telling them I was sorry to have bothered them; so well brought up! My parents chided me, but not too much. For they could not possibly have known how near to disaster I came, and I was not keen to enlighten them.

They knew nothing whatever about the next adventure, only four years later, for it occurred far from home. I was in Algiers at a very difficult and dangerous time, when the war between France and its colony was at its most virulent, becoming more and more vile as the end approached. People were routinely blown up in bus queues, or as they sipped coffee in a corner bar. The word 'terrorist' was not, as I recall, then used, though the recourse to terrorising the population and the occupying forces, who have all the arsenal of oppression (never called 'terror') at their disposal, was the same then as it is now. My position was especially privileged, as I was the guest of an Arab family in the kasbah, connections of mine through students at the University of Montpellier, which meant that all the inhabitants knew I was to be protected, it being a cardinal rule among Arab peoples that every effort must be exerted to accommodate the honoured guest. It was as if a public announcement had been made, but the news passed from mouth to mouth, I suppose, and I felt utterly safe at a time when any stranger would have had to be careful. I even participated in an Arab wedding as one of the bearers of gifts from the bride's family to the groom's, a long procession through the tightly packed alleys, with ululating women lining the route and others showering rose-petals over us from windows above. I carried a cushion.

Several things impressed me about that occasion, which lasted two whole days. One was that mealtimes were exclusively male affairs, that the women, having prepared and displayed the food, fled into invisibility before we sat down. Another was that I was expected to belch loudly to demonstrate my appreciation, and, not being able to, I responded to anguished glances from around the table by pressing out a dissembled cough and pretending it must have been a burp. The third was that the bride, escorted through the streets by a female relation on either side to make sure she did not bump into anything (her eyes had to be kept shut throughout the walk), did not meet her husband until her fate had been sealed; it was only after the ceremonies, in the privacy of their closet, that she was permitted to open her eyes and see whom she had married. All very odd to me, of course, but as normal as afternoon tea to them, and it almost always worked to the satisfaction of (even to the growth of love between) both parties.

The trouble was, I was so accustomed to feeling safe in the kasbah that I mistakenly assumed I would be safe anywhere, whereas, if I wandered beyond its confines into the larger city where I was not known to anyone, this was far from the case. I was anxious to see as much of the city as was permissible in a state of war, and took a bus-ride towards the outskirts, where I think there was a botanical garden of sorts. When I got off the bus, the man who had been sitting next to me, only a year or two older than myself, alighted as well, and struck up a conversation. We naturally spoke in French, I knowing no Arabic tongue, though it was clear he was himself an Arab. He gave me his name, which I now forget. We talked of history and politics, myself careful not to say anything provocative despite the fact that I was at the most provocative age, when one assumes one has all the answers and everyone else is wilfully obtuse. We walked farther away from the main road, I anxious not to displease and he presumably on his way home; whenever we reached his destination I would be able to prise myself away without causing offence. But we never did.

Suddenly I was aware that he had a knife in his hand. It was long and thin, and looked remarkably sharp to me. He touched the small of my back with it, in a way unnoticeable to any passer-by, and told me to walk on; he was leading me somewhere. We went into woodland behind some houses, up a slight incline, then sat on the leafy ground, the knife still poised. He then laid it down by his side (nobody was in view by this time) and proceeded to unbutton himself.

He quite clearly wanted sex, and I imagine he would have been satisfied with a minimal sort. Like most men in his culture, he had probably been denied all outlets long after he first felt the need to meet the demands of the sexual drive and would have to wait patiently for marriage, whenever that might arrive. But I was too petrified to reason, too paralysed by the certain knowledge that I was in a strange place, far from witnesses, with a man I did not know, who was armed, in a country in the grip of war and therefore of daily exposure to death. I felt I was doomed, that my end had come. It was useless, probably counter-productive, to shout. I resisted, with plaintive mien no doubt, and the knife was swiftly brought up to my neck, where I could feel its cold point. I used every ounce of effort not to tremble, for had I fled or fought, I should have been despatched in seconds, my body left to remain undiscovered probably for days, and even when found arousing little interest. My life depended on coolness; I remember clearly thinking this even as the nightmare was playing out. He must be given hope.

It has often been said that my strong point is explanation. That day I was grateful for the talent. I talked to him, showed him that I was not worth the fight. By this time he knew well enough that I was English, and possibly thought me a wimp; at that moment, he was right. I made an attempt at masturbation, not so clumsy as to have insulted and outraged him, but bad enough to demonstrate that I was not really adept. The knife relaxed, was kept in his hand but brought down by his side. He tried to force me into fellation, but gave up when he realised all pleasure in the act was about to be thwarted by my incompetence; as for me, there could be no question of arousal when terrified at the possibility of my imminent extinction (I have never understood those people who, apparently, are *exclusively* aroused by pushing themselves virtually to the point of death by self-strangulation, the two experiences, of life-force through ejaculation and death-wish through simulated unconsciousness, being mutually exclusive, but never mind). So I resorted to clarification, explanation. I showed that I was a useless tyro, quite unable to meet his requirements, and that he would do better to look elsewhere. I also managed to slip in the point that I was staying in the kasbah with people he might respect. I cannot claim to remember all that I said, but the upshot was that he walked me back to the bus-stop. It was after the bus moved off, and his back turned on me for ever, that the sweat broke out under my arms and in my palms. Had he been more excitable, I should have been finished. As it was, perhaps I was saved not so much by my talking as by his boredom. Which is not quite the same thing.

My third too-close encounter occurred thirty years later. I was sitting at my desk in Caithness Road towards six o'clock in the evening, finishing off some work before I would need to bathe and prepare for dinner. I was due to take Debo Devonshire to the Garrick Club. The front doorbell rang. I was expecting no one, and answered with some irritation at being interrupted. There, leaning against the porch, was a black man, not much more than twenty years old, with a thin beard lining the edge of his face and stopping to form a gap at his chin; I noticed this detail because it was so odd and startling. He said he wanted to speak to me. I asked him what about. He said, obviously planning that I should invite him in, that he would tell me inside. I pointed out that I had work to do, and made to apologise for closing the door. Then he said, ominously, 'I know who you are.' I had by that time written several newspaper articles on murder, and my book on the Nilsen case, *Killing for Company*, had been published a few years before. 'I want to talk to you,' he said. The conversation, though brief and banal, was beginning to edge towards threat.

When I asked the man who, then, I was, he was unable to say (so my books had nothing to do with this unexpected visit after all). There was a pause. I told him that I didn't know who he was, either. 'Yes, you do,' he snapped, almost in a whisper. I asked him to tell me his name, in the hope it might ring a bell, and he refused. 'Well, in that case,' I said, 'I really can't help you, and I do have some work to get on with. Sorry!' And I gently, not rudely, closed the door.

A few minutes later, the doorbell rang again. Of course I knew it must be the stranger, but, stupidly no doubt, I felt sorry for him, because he must be frustrated at my not having the courtesy to ask him in. Yes, naïve, I know, but it is a foolishness which derives from my almost obsessive reliance upon reason; I thought I could *talk* to him, and then everything would be fine. This time, I was horribly wrong.

'So you don't know me,' he said. 'That's right,' I began. 'If only you'd give me a clue, and tell me what you want, I might be able to . . .' But I could not finish the sentence. His right fist came flying towards my face, and hit me hard on the left cheek. I felt nothing, but saw him turn on his heel and run faster than I thought was possible for a man with only two legs. Then I closed the door again, as if in self-protection (not much reasoning in *that*, one might add). All this within three seconds. I saw blood on the wallpaper just inside the door, and touched my face. It was wet and warm. I ran to the bathroom and looked. Half my cheek was hanging open, the blood pouring out in soft flows, like lava down a mountain-side. I stuffed a towel against my face in an attempt to stem the haemorrhage, and it quickly became sodden. Now my face was beginning to throb. I grabbed another towel. Why a mere punch, however powerful, could cause such damage I only discovered later. Between the third and fourth knuckles of his hand the man had concealed a Stanley-knife, of the sort used to cut carpets. He had obviously placed it there, with harsh and firm purpose, between his first and second visits to my front door. My face had been sliced open like a slab of Parma ham.

The rest of that evening was both funny and relaxed, but for different reasons. Maybe Nature has a way of ensuring calm the better to face impending catastrophe, as one is said to fall numb before a tiger about to attack (which is why, so I am told, animals are not hurt when they are caught as prey by other animals, the body seeing to that). In addition to which, I had a way of deflecting misery by denying it. I first telephoned for an ambulance, and was told to stay calm (which I already was) and breathe deeply; the ambulance would be with me in minutes. Then I telephoned Debo. I remember thinking that it was not acceptable to stand a lady up, even with half my face hanging off, that I had to warn her not to go to dinner and find me absent; I also reflected, bizarrely, that had I been Italian I might not have bothered.

It was difficult to talk. My lips would not meet to frame the words articulately, and the blood still oozed. Debo later told me that what was most frightening was my panting, so I suppose I was not as self-possessed as I imagined, unless panting be merely the audible echo of pulse. I said only what was necessary, and rang off. The ambulance arrived.

I was treated inside the ambulance, and seen immediately upon arrival in casualty at Charing Cross Hospital (in the Fulham Palace Road). The surgeon, a young New Zealander, made an initial examination and asked me if I had had anything to eat. I told him I had had a cup of tea and a biscuit at about five o'clock, an hour before the attack. 'That's a pity,' he said, ' 'cos I can't operate for at least another four hours, and meanwhile the blood won't stop flowing.' I knew that myself, because I kept having to empty my mouth to prevent myself from swallowing it. 'There's only one thing for it, mate, I'm going to have to seal those arteries in your cheek now, close them up in other words, so the blood can't get out. Now, the knife has cut through three arteries, so you're going to have to hold tight while I do them one after the other. They won't be used again, but don't worry, you've got far more arteries in your cheeks than you need, so you won't miss them. But I've got to do it without general anaesthetic. I can't put you to sleep because of that damn biscuit.'

I then had the odd experience of watching, fully conscious, as hands and instruments came down before my eyes towards my face and into it, and tiny pin-pricks of local anaesthetic were followed by major plumbing, all of which, despite those pin-pricks, I felt. It was not excruciating, but it was peculiar and uncomfortable. Once more, I think Nature has its own mysterious insurance against pain. I only wanted to co-operate, and do the surgeon a favour by being compliant.

I then lay on a bed in a ward as the lights went down and I stared at the ceiling, waiting for those hours to pass. In a little while, a figure came walking down the corridor towards me (my bed was opposite the door to the ward, and I could see far). To my astonishment, it was Nunc Willcox, the Chairman of the Garrick Club. Debo had telephoned to cancel our table, and told the doorman who answered the phone that something terrible had happened to me, she knew not what exactly, but that I had been 'slashed'. Richard then went to announce the fact to the Long Table. The Chairman, about to start his dinner, immediately got up and took a cab to Charing Cross Hospital. Even more delightfully, he said, 'You're lucky it's only me here. I had to stop the rest of the table from coming.' That visit, as well as Debo's concern, enabled me to face the operation with something almost akin to pleasure.

That allows me the opportunity to explain, as best I can, the singular nature of club friendships. When I had been growing up, I thought, like all young people discovering their first shafts of wisdom, that the world was divided into friends and acquaintances. Friends, whom one knew intimately, and to whom one told one's troubles, amounted to four or five individuals, if one was lucky. Acquaintances, with whom one enjoyed an occasional dinner but who were nowhere near privy to one's secrets and one's real self, might number twenty or thirty. It was only when I was elected to the Garrick Club that I realised there was a third category of which I had been entirely ignorant. Club friends are not intimate or inquisitorial, they neither seek nor deflect confidences but rather regard them as outside their remit, yet they are far more than acquaintances, for they carry an unspoken and utterly improbable bond (not duty, far from that) of loyalty. I had known Nunc for years, but only within the walls of the club; he had not been to my house, nor I to his. We knew nothing of one another's personal life. Yet my lying in hospital as the result of an attack was far more important to him than his dinner. He was, by the way, my only visitor in the two days I was on the ward.

The surgeon explained that I would have a scar for the rest of my life, but that the Stanley-knife had ensured that it would be a neat one. 'If it had been a bottle, you would have been in a right state.' He then gave me the cheerful news, 'I may not be the best stitcher in the hospital, but I'm the only one on duty tonight, so it's me you've got.'

When I went home two days later, I called the police and told them the story. They made house-to-house enquiries, but nobody had seen anything, and there appeared to be no record of a man fitting his description on their lists. They were sympathetic, but obviously thought me erratically stupid to have opened the door twice. They could adduce no motive for the assault. My own theory is that he was (or more likely had been) a local person who had seen the swags and tails at the front window often enough, had assumed that there might be money in such a house, and had made a bold attempt to finger his way in, which had failed. He struck out of corrosive annoyance with himself as much as with me.

When I was able to reflect later, I recognised that I had escaped with a scar, which, centimetres off target in any direction, might have blinded me, or killed me; that Stanley-knife cutting through veins in the neck would have done damage which even the best New Zealand stitcher could not have remedied. That thought made me shudder.

I imagined for about twenty-four hours that I could no longer go to the greengrocer without an escort, and that I must take taxis everywhere, as that man knew where I lived and would always know it. The one place in the world where I was the least safe was my own home. I soon dismissed the thought as unworthy. I would not change my routines nor smother my spirit for a stranger with a grudge. He was never caught.

Had I plunged down the cliff at Barry, had the Algerian kidnapper persisted in his desire to force me, had the Stanley-knifer been less accurate, then my history since would not have been there to record. It is an odd, wavering thought that runs through my head every time I hear of or read about untimely death, and it has troubled me deeply whenever I have written about the people who have caused these premature finalities – Nilsen, Dahmer, Frederick West and so on. They have placed a full-stop where a comma ought to have happened, have closed something that was open, have wrapped, pocketed and burnt somebody else's future. I find this worse than the gruesomely violent act of murder itself, and my pity is most excited by the black curtain which cancels hope. That is why I detest murderers, and also loathe those political figures, past and present, who trample on life by a decision taken at a desk, and murder at a distance.

There was one occasion on which I experienced the blank nothingness of non-life – le néant – although 'experience' is hardly the correct verb, there being no consciousness to do the experiencing. It would be more accurate to say that 'it' experienced me, for I was entirely the passive receptor. I had been out late with a group of American tourists, finishing with a vile dinner at one of those establishments invented for the tourist with no imagination of his own, where one wears funny hats and sings funny songs in order to be part of 'history'. This one was called The Elizabethan, somewhere in Kensington, and as it has long since closed I am not nervous about insulting it. By candlelight, and with Henry VIII presiding, we ate, from earthenware bowls, soup without spoons and bread flung across the tables, and drank, from earthenware jugs, the most revolting cheap wine ever to disgrace a table. I was responsible for the whole bunch, and had to get them out to the airport the following morning for a return flight to the United States. There were about two hundred of them, due to fly out on different flights to different US destinations, for which I hired buses allocated to each flight. We drank too much of that filth, and I was not home until after two in the morning.

At 7.00 a.m. I was back at the hotel to supervise this complicated departure. The strain was physical and mental, for I was heavily overhung and tired, and carried too many details in my head. In the street, beside one of the buses, I suddenly found myself sprawled on the ground, with no memory of having fallen. I struggled to my feet, brushed myself down, and got on with the job, thinking that I would go straight back to bed when all this was over. Then it happened again. It must have taken three seconds for me to fall and recover, three seconds of what was total black-out. Over the next quarter of an hour, I was subjected to the same temporary collapse half a dozen times. At last the buses all departed for their separate flights, and I shrugged with real relief, about to call a cab and go home. Then a middle-aged couple appeared from inside the hotel and asked where their bus was; I had allowed it to go without the full complement of passengers, and these two were stranded, anxious to get to the airport in time. I remember no more that day.

I woke up in hospital some hours later. I had apparently fallen to the ground again, this time in the grip of a full epileptic fit, arms and legs thrashing, mouth foaming, a terrible sight to behold. It was a porter at the hotel who alerted the manager and called an ambulance, but I did not seek to discover whether they had had to hold me down and prevent my tongue from furling backwards down my throat. I was thirty-two years old and had never suffered a fit before.

In hospital I was given the Happy Drug, which I have spent the rest of my life trying to deserve again; it sent me into the most blissful state as I was wheeled on a stretcher down the corridor, and I told the nurse pushing me that she was the most beautiful girl in the world. I was treated in some way, then had dozens of wires attached to my scalp in an effort to determine whether I was in danger of falling victim to epilepsy in the future. I was told that it could happen to anyone at all, that some people have to tolerate several fits a day, and others have one every few years. Some people never have another. I was given pills which I would have to take every day for the rest of my life.

About two weeks later I threw the pills away. I could not abide the idea of being a slave to chemicals for ever, and diagnosed myself as having been under too much strain for the brain to cope with all at once. My neurons had gone on strike. And I would make sure that in future I limited myself to the best Burgundy. I have never suffered a fit since, the only echo of that event being those tiny involuntary ripples of leg-jerking in bed as I am trying to sink into the arms of Morpheus. I sometimes think that for a few hours I was non-existent save as an inert body, all conscious cognition stolen from me, as if unliving (hardly the same as 'dead'). It is not the same as an unconsciousness induced by anaesthesia, for that is controlled and deliberate. This was more like snipping the cord of life, making a firm rupture, ceasing to be anything more than a breathing machine. It is a customary truism to say that every-one hopes death will be as sudden as this, an abrupt passage from being to non-being without the painful, frightening knowledge of what is happening. I do not agree. I shall cherish the time to take my leave, for once using time as my servant, and not myself being its slave. I hope that is what Nature has in store.

CHAPTER THREE

A Murderer in the Family, and Ballet

Writing about the diseased and distorted minds of addictive murderers, as I now have done three times, has brought me more than my share of anguish at the woeful cruelties which lie at the potential of human behaviour. But it has also brought unexpected softness close to the source of these miseries. For every vile murderer has a family, and the members of his immediate family are not only as horrified by his crimes as the rest of us, but have to bear the awful knowledge that his warped personality might have been, to one degree or another, shaped by them. He may even be like them in essence, and that element of his character which went disastrously off-course may be recognisable within their own hearts. It is a fiercely unsettling reflection, and I have come across many different ways of coping with it, all of them touching and surprising.

The bravest was Dr Lionel Dahmer, Ph.D., the father of Milwaukee killer Jeffrey Dahmer, who had drugged and strangled seventeen young men, dismembered them, bleached their bones and kept their skulls (even the entire skeletons of two of them), and who, when arrested in 1991, was found to be living with a human head on a plate in the refrigerator, various organs stuck at the bottom of the freezer, a filing-cabinet of bones, and two bodies, one on his bed and another in the bathtub, over which he had to step when taking a shower. On the day this nightmare ended, and police arrested him in his stinking apartment, freely admitting they were stunned by what they discovered, the telephone rang. It was Lionel, calling from his laboratory in Pittsburgh. He wanted to know if anything had happened to his son. It could never have occurred to him that Jeff had caused something hideous to happen to other people. The shock, when he was eventually told (not on the telephone, thank God), was such that he never fully recovered.

Lionel was a soft-spoken, gentle, gentlemanly, diffident man, with a quiet, compulsive niceness which was never declamatory or exposed. One could not speak of his 'charm', because that indefinable quality at least requires some effort to announce itself. Lionel was like a somnolent labrador, perfectly pleasant but difficult to arouse. Apparently he was liable to be excited, mildly, only by the Wimbledon Lawn Tennis Championships. It would be difficult to imagine any-one for whom this catastrophe would be a crueller blow.

Lionel was an industrial chemist who worked far from home (Pennsylvania on weekdays, home in Ohio at weekends), married to his second wife, Shari. Jeffrey and his younger brother had been issue of the first marriage, which had broken up when Jeffrey was seventeen. But the boy's disintegration had begun long before this (and his brother did not suffer from the divorce in any discernible way), and Lionel had to face the fact that his son had been a devil-in-the-making even as he was growing into adolescence. For it was then that Jeffrey had first shown interest in the corpses of animals found on country roads, and had asked his father to instruct him on how to disconnect the skeleton and re-assemble it. Strangely only in the light of what we know now, but understandably in the light of what Lionel then knew about his son, he was elated. For Jeff had never been interested in anything. He was blank, amorphous, featureless, a child apart, who hardly smiled, spoke in a monotone (or not at all), did not mix well, shrank from contact, and promised to fail in life. Now at last he had found an interest, an enthusiasm, and it was something that Lionel, as a scientist, could help him with. He felt, in fact, that Jeffrey might grow up to become a scientist like himself. The dissection of corpses was a worthy step in the right direction.

After Jeffrey's arrest, Lionel was forced to recognise that his whole life as a father had been a mistake. Worse than this, that Jeffrey's descent into his private hell had begun with a pathological quietness, an apartness, a separation from the back-slapping bonhomie of his contemporaries which was precisely the same defect of personality from which he, Lionel, had suffered all his life. Jeffrey was not an inexplicable aberration; he was definitely Lionel's mirror. As if this were not enough, Lionel was also deeply religious, a creationist who was prone to interpret the Bible literally and to think and feel the Bible's imagery of Black and White to be correct. His son's hideous crime could only mean one thing – that he had sired the Devil.

The fact that he was not crushed by this he owed to the support of his wife Shari. I got to know them very well during Jeffrey's trial, and have visited them since. As I pointed out in *Getting Personal*, it was Shari Dahmer who made contact with me after I had been interviewed on television, which perhaps made the relationship more secure. She and Lionel had not been hunted and caught (indeed, nobody knew where they were staying in Milwaukee, or whether they were smuggled in from somewhere distant). I had seen them pass through a rear entrance to the courtroom, through the offices of the forensic psychiatrist, where I sat both before and after each session in court, and I had not approached them. They sat at the back of the court, mysterious, unfathomable, impenetrable, dignified. Not for a second did they succumb to the prevailing American habit of bursting into tears in public, presumably as a badge of one's humanity, a proof that one is 'in touch with' one's emotions. (Some of the victims had families much less resistant to fashion, who became lachrymose, even hysterical, as soon as a television camera pointed at them.) It was only in private, later, that I saw just how much Lionel had been hurt by the public display of his own tragedy as his son's conduct was pitilessly scrutinised in court (as indeed it had to be).

I did not see Lionel weep; he was too contained a person to allow that to happen. But I did see how much he depended upon Shari's strength to support him, and I have no difficulty in imagining that he might have given way to his distress with her, and with her alone. She often answered when he was groping for the words to express the inexpressible, or for those other words to convey his sorrow and regret without abusing his son. She did not interrupt, or attempt to speak for him, but she intervened rather than allow a silence to pile its insinuations upon all three of us. She was support and solace. He was lucky to have her by his side.

They were entirely opposite in appearance and manner. While Lionel could have disappeared into the smallest of crowds and become invisible in a trice, Shari was big, bold, blatant, conspicuous. Merely physically she was a larger specimen, being taller than her husband, and, though not fat, definitely fleshy. We used to laugh at the fact that whenever she and I embraced, my face would be lost between her breasts, and it was a measure of her security and serenity that she never resented the laughter or interpreted it as a personal slight. She wore bright red lipstick on lips which frequently spread into the broadest smile, or frank laughter. With a great rush of hair to top it all, she reminded one of Dolly Parton, though without the latter's loudness or vulgarity. Shari was generous in the deployment of her ample personality, but not insensitive. She had the warmest of hearts and the finest of instincts. I felt she was secretly glad that she had no blood connection with Jeffrey, but, of course, she was never so crass as to say so. Her job was to make sure that her husband did not crumple beneath the

69

knowledge that he had the closest possible connection to a young man who had bored holes into the scalps of drugged, living people in the mad hope of thereby making them his personal zombies.

Lionel eventually exorcised his painful anxieties by publishing a book, A Father's Story, as candid and honest and dignified as the man himself, which was remarkable considering that it was ghosted. He had originally asked me to write it for him, an invitation I reluctantly declined because I thought it would interfere with my own analysis of the case. I should have liked to have been able to help, for he was not somebody one could easily abandon. I saw the Dahmers again after Jeffrey had been killed by a fellow inmate in prison. They were relieved the ordeal was over, not for themselves, but for their son, who they knew had suffered the torment of implacable remorse. (Personally, I wondered whether he was capable of it, but it was obviously important Lionel should be convinced that he was.) We now barely exchange Christmas cards, which does not match my fondness for them, and, I think, theirs for me. Thus from such an unlikely event as a trial for murder in Milwaukee may human contact of some warmth emerge.

It emerged, too, in Scotland, where in 1983 it fell to me to have to explain to a white-haired, garrulous and gullible old lady exactly what her son Dennis had done when trusting young men were enticed into his den. Dennis Nilsen had been charged with murder, and was suspected of having killed fifteen people (it was more likely to have been twelve). He had intended to plead guilty at his trial, which would have obviated the need for police to present all their evidence, and the precise nature of his quite ghastly crimes would have been kept away from public knowledge. But, he was prevailed upon at the last minute to change his plea, and the trial would last up to three weeks. It was due to start on a Monday. I realised that his mother, Betty Scott, who lived with her second husband Adam in the small town of Strichen in Aberdeenshire, where Dennis had grown up, would read the details of the case against her son in the daily newspapers on Tuesday. She knew only that he had killed people. How, or why, or what he had done to them after death, of all this she knew nothing. I could not tolerate that she should discover news of such profound importance to her psyche as part of the public's daily dose of entertainment. So I went up to Scotland on Sunday to tell her myself.

I had met her before, of course. She had always made me welcome, cooked meals for me, brewed endless cups of tea, all the while knowing that I intended to expose Dennis's troubled personality in print. She hoped it would help him. She certainly could not. Mother and son had had very little contact since he had set up home in London many years before. She did not understand him, and he made no allowance for her, whom he thought limited and simple. Well, she was, but she was a great deal more genuine and decent than he was. There was a real glow of humanity in her voice and in her sweet smile, and even if she did talk too much, it was never with intent to deceive. Dennis Nilsen, on the other hand, though he spoke with enviable fluency and hard intellectual grasp, was determined that words should obfuscate rather than clarify. He never said anything in which one could trace the cool thread of truth. Since he was factual and objective in the information he offered, it was a huge problem for me, when writing my book on his case, to disentangle psychological mendacity from factual truth, in other words to work out, not whether what he was saying was correct or not, but why he had chosen that particular piece of information to impart at that particular time. He was ever a secret strategist. So to listen to his mother's blissfully uncomplicated chatter was like smelling apple-blossom after trudging through mud.

A trust grew between us which I frankly cherished. Betty Scott was so sweet-natured that I felt protective towards her, and made it my business to recover all her family snapshots of Dennis as a boy which had been snatched from her hands by greedy pressmen and sold throughout the world for gold. I looked forward to visiting her as respite from the sordid business of studying Nilsen's homosexual necrophilia and technique of dismemberment, of which she knew nothing whatever.

Then came that Sunday when I had to explain to her, in front of the fire in a cosy council sitting-room in Strichen, matters which no mother should ever have to face. Betty was so guileless that she vouchsafed to me the devastating fact that, of all her seven children, Dennis had been the only one she could not cuddle, could not pick up and fondle, quite unaware that this kind of non-tactile relationship could easily have contributed to his retreat into selfish love. I could not bring myself to make this point to her (why pile further bewilderment upon her fragile old shoulders?), but I know for certain that if she were to read these words now, she would harbour no anger or resentment. I was proud to know such an ordinary woman. And Nilsen was perceptibly uncomfortable that she and I should get along so well together. The anger was all in him, the accommodation and tolerance all in her. This realisation made it finally possible for me not to blame her for having kept him, as an infant, at a distance, as one should in all logic, but to chastise *him*. For once, my close reasoning gave way to an emotional or intuitive grasp of what was real, namely that there must have been something wrong with Dennis Nilsen from the very beginning. If this is close to suggesting that a devilish nature is sometimes innate, a notion which runs starkly contrary to everything I have tried to maintain in my professional life, then so be it.

This irrational conviction is the fruit of friendship with Betty Scott. Not all truths can necessarily be seized head-on; some may be attained through serpentine and unlikely avenues.

*   *   *

My friendship with dancers in the Royal Ballet, and with Doreen Wells in particular, tangentially led me to some moments of personal hilarity and others of potential historical interest in the ballet world. Among the former was my ludicrous command of the conductor's baton.

I spent many months hovering on the fringes of the Royal Ballet's touring section, devoted to bringing full-length ballets to small towns throughout Britain which had never, or rarely, seen them. I sat in on many a rehearsal, and many a private class given by Erling Sunde, especially to the promising seventeen-year-old David Wall, who was being trained to dance the lead in *Swan Lake* (and who would eventually surge towards a glittering international career). It was a fascinating privilege, and I was grateful to the Director, John Field, for tolerating my presence so easily. In retrospect, there can hardly seem any reason why he should. I contributed nothing.

The resident conductor was Ashley Lawrence, a lonely but adorable man of rugged feature and gentle manner, whom I often discovered dining alone in a restaurant, when all the dancers tended to dine together as one extended family. He, too, accepted my frequent presence at orchestral rehearsals, when privacy and concentration might have been expected to exclude any stranger, and we frequently joked about how well I knew the music from having heard it so often. Until one afternoon when I foolishly boasted (and not seriously, I must add) that if ever he felt fed up I could take over and conduct the orchestra for him.

He handed me the baton, and challenged me to do just that.

The orchestra, bless them, grinning broadly, made no objection. Not for the first time in my life, I wished I had kept my mouth shut. Yet the temptation to take the baton pulled me one way, while the expectation of making a fool of myself kept my pulse beating with the fury of fear. It could not, surely, be that difficult.

Knowing the music, I found out, was not the clue. *Anticipating* it was the secret. In front of the mirror at home, I could simply match the music and do brilliantly. With a live orchestra, waiting for my instructions, and only responding to the down-beat of my arm, it was quite another matter. The *tempi* and noises I produced were catastrophic, chaotically surprising to me and desperately amusing to the musicians. The embarrassing nightmare seemed to last ten minutes, but on reflection, I know it could not have done. It was probably all over in two minutes and a torrent of mirth. For months afterwards, I could not pass a musician in the corridor without receiving a knowing smirk of recognition.

The young Kenneth MacMillan was a shy, deferential man, with a manner so self-effacing that one might imagine him to be assistant office organiser rather than one of the towering geniuses of twentieth-century British choreography. He rarely spoke above a whisper, and I could not picture him shouting his instructions at recalcitrant dancers; indeed, I learned that he never did, but politely suggested they could do the step the way he would attempt to show them. It was well-known that MacMillan's method was as boldly different from Frederick Ashton's as their resulting ballets were sharply contrasted in style. While Fred would go to the rehearsal room and tell his dancers to 'do something', effectively monitoring their own creative impulses and choosing, with his impeccable eye, those which worked best, Kenneth prepared meticulously for months, so that when he turned up for rehearsal he would know in advance exactly what he wanted and how he was going to get it. Both, of course, tailored the shape and style of their inventions to suit the bodies and talents of the dancers pre-selected to be their muse, but Fred did so on the spot, and Kenneth in his head.

Kenneth's especial muse was Lynn Seymour, the wonderfully dramatic Canadian dancer for whom he had already created many ballets, *The Invitation* among them, with its frighteningly graphic rape scene of a young virgin by a much older married man; the girl, having been violated, slides slowly down the man's body, passing his knees, to an exhausted crumple on the floor. It was shocking to audiences more familiar with swans pretending to be young women and princesses going to sleep for a hundred years. Kenneth undoubtedly wanted to shock. He wanted to put upon the stage his own tortured, painful vision of human life skewed by a world of competing selfishnesses, with its guaranteed harvest of misery and hurt, and was determined to show that classical ballet was a proper medium to cope with such a subject. In fact, he succeeded so well that it began to look as if classical ballet was hopeless at conveying fairy-tale happiness, and had been wasting its potential for a century or more. He created a new art within an established art-form.

By the time I knew him, MacMillan was already well known for his gritty, demanding, intense ballets, wherein even a com-paratively gentle theme of loneliness, as *Solitaire*, made one leave the theatre feeling upset. But they had all been ballets in one act. He had not yet attempted a full-length three-act ballet, so the news that he was working on a new production of *Romeo and Juliet* to Prokoviev's score caused much excitement and anticipation. I was introduced to him by his best friend Georgina Parkinson, a lusciously dark-eyed beautiful ballerina who had shared a flat with Doreen when they both started in the Company (her husband, the photographer Roy Round, composed a portrait of her which was a picture of her eyes, framed on all sides by the black feathers of a fan). MacMillan himself was not yet married. He did not seem the sort who ever would be, for his teeming intellectual life, forever thinking and inwardly seeing, left no room for shared pleasures. That would change when he met Deborah some years later.

I invited Kenneth to dinner at my flat in Mecklenburgh Square in 1964, together with Georgina and Roy, and it was probably my biggest culinary disaster ever (although there have been other occasions to compete). I cooked a continental stew, packed with taste, which included tender meat chunks, vegetables, herbs, spices, a number of which one could only find, in those gastronomically impoverished days, in one shop in Soho, wine and stock. The intention was to serve this delicious mixture with some pasta, also bought in Soho. Unfortunately, I forgot to put the liquid stock into the mix, so that when I smelt a suspiciously strong whiff of burning metal, and saw the bowl of stock standing neglected by the stove, I realised that my lovely stew would have to be scraped from the side of the cooking-pot with gardening tools. We ate pasta with butter!

The conversation touched inevitably upon *Romeo and Juliet* and I discovered that Kenneth's habit was to listen to the score over and over again, all day long, whatever else he might be doing as well, as the picture suggested by the music gradually formed itself in his imagination to the point where no other choreography would do but the one which insisted (and which he, by a process of thought, feeling, mood, had conjured into existence).

Once, when I was visiting him at his flat in Seymour Street near Marble Arch, he told me something I then thought astonishing. The record-player was on as usual, and the music was soaring to the ceiling. It was that most impassioned section wherein the entire orchestra, goaded by straining strings, fills the heart with a longing burst of emotion and unease, every musician playing for all he's worth to convey Prokoviev's overwhelming surges towards a climax which yet lies hidden. In the text, it comes at the moment when Juliet is at a terrible crossroads in her young life. Her family is forcing her to marry Paris, whom she visibly detests (MacMillan here created a dance in which the suitor lifts her and she wriggles free, her manifest distaste for his embrace forming part of the choreographic invention), and she is in love with Romeo, who has killed her brother in retaliation for his slaughter of Romeo's close friend Mercutio. She is alone on stage, alone with her thoughts and her distress, and doesn't know which way to turn.

To anyone else, the music would suggest a wrenching, violent solo for the ballerina, for it sang with such an eloquence that the dance must surely strive to match it. Kenneth said he had decided Juliet should, at that point, do nothing.

It was a bold, on the face of it a foolhardy, idea. At the first night, one saw what he meant. Juliet sits on the edge of her bed, still, reflecting, deciding, doubting, fearing, while the music surges out from the pit. She seems to be there for long minutes; I have never timed it, but for a ballerina to sit still when music seems to be urging her to get up, even one minute is an eternity. What Kenneth showed was that a dancer was also an actress (just as Maria Callas was not just a singer), and that it was possible for her to demonstrate, through the tautness of limbs which were not in repose but waiting to spring, the agony of decision. In the hands of Lynn Seymour, it was a moment of intense drama, the music apparently doing all the work, but Lynn making us see her fearsome anguish. The scene terminates with her rushing off the stage, cloak flying behind, to see Friar Lawrence, and we know, then, what she has been through in the last minutes. The cliché is permissible – it was a stroke of genius.

Much to Kenneth's annoyance, Lynn Seymour and Christopher Gable, for whom he had created the ballet, were not allowed to dance until a much later performance, opening night being reserved for the acknowledged stars of the Royal Ballet, Margot Fonteyn and Rudolf Nureyev. Both dancers of unique quality, and arguably the finest partnership in the world at the time, but both horribly unsuited to *Romeo and Juliet*.

Nevertheless, history very quickly showed that the ballet belonged to Seymour and Gable, whose youth, drama and despair haunted the stage throughout, while the Fonteyn/Nureyev partnership returned to its glitter and has not been historically associated with this ballet at all. Lynn's visceral response to the tragedy she had to portray betokened not only raw emotional reality, but a huge intelligence. She was a woman who lived thoroughly, and demonstrated in her performance the lessons which life had taught her. Next to her, most ballerinas were pretty and beguiling, gorgeous in technique, delicate and fragile in its application, devoted above all to the beauty of form. And it is true, the beauty of form has its own eloquence and can enable an audience to glimpse truth through unaccustomed radiance. But for Lynn Seymour, as for Kenneth MacMillan, ballet was but dumb entertainment unless it touched the core of human apprehensions and anxieties. That is why she was the perfect ballerina to convey his vision, he the perfect choreographer to realise her genius.

The private character of ballet-dancers nearly always mirrors the intensity of their stage performance. Lynn was a strong person, unresponsive to supine admiration, unlikely to be hoodwinked, laconic and abrupt when she detected insincerity, a woman who did not suffer fools or flatterers. She heartily distrusted the press and was reluctant to grant interviews.

She also used sharp Billingsgate language when the occasion required. This was no retiring English rose, but a blunt antagonist when roused.

On the other hand, those ballerinas who dance with an eye to precision and obedience are often fragile creatures, bereft of that wide scope of understanding which a full and searching education offers. Having devoted their lives to the dance, they have literally had little time for anything else (class in the morning, rehearsal in the afternoon, performance in the evening), and have both a limited view of the world in which they live and the people who surround them, and a poor chance of withstanding the disappointments, deceptions and cruelties which must beset them as they beset anyone else. Their world is so closed, and so rooted in make-believe that, unless they find a resource within themselves which is independent of the demands their blinkered training makes upon them, they risk folding as soon as unfair reality intrudes upon them. There are no magic wands in the real world, no Lilac Fairy to make everything turn out all right in the end.

The number who succumb is abnormally high. The famous case of Spessivtseva is perhaps an exaggeration, but she is a brooding example. One of the glories of the Russian dance in the 1930s, and by some accounts the greatest interpreter of *Giselle* in the twentieth century, Olga Spessivtseva, finally so infected with the comforting unrealities of her pretend world, lost her mind completely and spent her last years in a mental institution. Even among the dancers I knew there were always worrying signs of chronic instability, provoked not only by the escape from truth, but by back-stage jealousies, competition, and the awful realisation that their professional lives would come to an end, over thirty-five for men, over forty for women, just as other 'ordinary' people were reaching their prime. Tellingly, those who endure are the ones who make an easy transition into character roles dependent upon mime, tradition, and long experience (Gerd Larsen, Leslie Edwards, Derek Rencher and so on), and these are precisely the dancers who draw upon a native intelligence which protects them from the dangers of the world they have embraced.

I have known some to commit suicide, either with brutal deliberation, or through the gradual disintegration of abuse. One young man, whom I did not know very well and whose motives I cannot therefore properly assess, was Adrian Reynolds, unheard-of, unremembered, unlisted in the reference books, because he was only in the *corps de ballet* of what was then called the Festival Ballet (now the English National Ballet). He was, I think, twenty-one when he swallowed enough sleeping-pills washed down with Ribena to end his life. Moreover, he chose a place and a time when he knew his body would not be discovered until it was far too late. He went to his parents' house in the suburbs of London while they were away on holiday, touring in a caravan and utterly unlocatable. Nobody knew he had gone there (I believe he was estranged from them, possibly due to his choice of career), or where they lived. He was, one might say, too young to have suffered the doubts and disorientations inherent in the dancer's life, but perhaps he saw them coming. Who knows? I mention Adrian because, though he knew me only as an acquaintance and neighbour, when his will was opened it was discovered that I was named as executor.

He had taken out insurance only a couple of months before his suicide, which indicated, to me at least, that he had been planning this disaster for some time. That suggested he felt himself to be a disappointment and disgrace and thought his provision of funds would somehow compensate for his lack of promise. But I am only guessing. He left no note, no clue; it was my first experience as an executor, and I was faced with the heart-breaking task of having to collect all his assets, everything that belonged to him, and remove them into my care until such time as the deceased's intentions could be carried out. His parents pleaded with me to let them keep a long-playing record, some remembrance of their only son, and I despised myself for having to follow the strict legal path and execute the will correctly. I was young myself, in my late twenties, and fearful of getting it wrong. I now know better, of course, and would happily distribute bits and pieces to friends before authority pounced. It can do no harm, unless there are disputes. One of the most awful days of my life was when I had to bring Mr and Mrs Reynolds together with Petrus Bosman, the man Adrian had lived with, and read out his final intentions. Petrus was almost the sole beneficiary. I felt like a thief.

The Reynolds bore no grudge. They appreciated Petrus, and sought not to make him feel guilty. He probably came to some private arrangement with them when my work was done. By an odd coincidence, another dancer who killed himself, albeit not so deliberately, had also lived with Petrus. This was Graham Usher, who rose to be a Principal of the Royal Ballet, was the starring lead in Ashton's *La Fille Mal Gardée* and one of the greatest exponents of the Bluebird *pas-de-deux* in his generation, but who saw it all coming to an end far too soon and could not cope with having not an uncertain future, but on the contrary, a future which was guaranteed to be empty.

Graham was typical of the local boy who soared. From a modest family in Yorkshire, his horizons would have been severely curtailed by circumstances had it not been for the accidental discovery of his talent. (It is astonishing, by the way, how many of the world's great dancers have come to ballet by chance. Natalia Makarova did not respond to an exigent inner driving-force that would brook no obstacle, but was walking down the street in Leningrad [St Petersburg] one day, saw the

Vaganova School and wondered what it was. The teachers who received the little girl's enquiry immediately spotted her build and shape, grabbed her, and decided the fate that would eventually lead her to international stardom. The little boy who became Wayne Sleep went to the doctor with a complaint of flat feet. The medication recommended to his parents was a course in elementary ballet, and the feet went on to do faster *entrechats* than anyone else in the world.) Graham Usher took up dancing because he was not much good at anything else and nobody knew what to do with him.

From the start, he was not at ease in the spotlight. He had a markedly effeminate manner (contrary to public assumptions, this is rare in the ballet world), and years of being teased and mocked in Yorkshire had left permanent wounds. He had subconsciously proceeded to see himself as others saw him, and consequently hated being noticed, picked out, remarked upon, the very antithesis of those peacock qualities required for a career on the stage. He assumed he was always being criticised, and he defended himself, from very early in his progress to the top, with the bravado of cigarettes and drink in fashionable, but for an unsophisticated Yorkshire lad, dangerous quantities.

(Another aside: far more dancers smoke and drink than one might imagine. Makarova used to smoke up to sixty cigarettes a day at the height of her career, sometimes snatching one in the wings between a *pas-de-deux* and her solo. She gave up totally after her retirement from the stage. Lucette Aldous, the miniature, perky, pretty Australian ballerina whose head seemed to be at the level of everyone else's shoulders, could happily drink a bottle of whisky after a performance.)

Graham could not cope with the social life which fame brought to him, for he knew he had nothing much to say, and would say it in a manner which others might deride behind his back. Not that he was quiet; on the contrary, he was garrulous to a degree, but this was also defensive, filling the space that might otherwise be available for criticism. He was brilliant on stage, exciting, mercurial, stylish, manly. Off-stage, he knew quite well that he was none of these things. His rosebud lips, which reminded one of (female) silent-film stars, while they were not contrived by him, but were simply part of his genetic endowment, let him down when he was seen 'in real life' as it were. I am sure he would have preferred his many fans to see him on stage only and to have forgone the pleasure of waiting for him at the stage-door. And he would have preferred to stay at home and not be seen in society. He would have been lonelier, but he would have been safer, too.

Unfortunately, going out was part of a young man's life, and when he was living with Petrus, he could not refuse to go out all the time (occasionally he did) without causing offence. So the cigarettes accompanied him as prop, and the drinking increased. He never returned home without being wobbly with alcohol. At class the next morning he would have to sweat it all out. I never knew anyone who sweated so much. And this he did without complaint, for Graham was a very hard worker, with the stamina and strength of any navvy. His effeminate manner belied the power of his determination.

I once saw Graham's discomfiture and vulnerability at first hand, and may have awkwardly been the indirect source of it. He and Doreen Wells were due to dance a performance of *La Fille Mal Gardée* in Cardiff, and my parents lived nearby in Barry. I proposed to go down to Barry and get a ticket for my mother, who was unaccustomed to going anywhere. I told Graham, who asked whether perhaps he could stay, thus saving on the cost of a hotel room. I said yes first, then thought about it after-wards. My parents had *never* had a house-guest, and though my mother would be shy, I knew my father would be petrified. So I did not ask them, I told them after the event. There was a spare bed in the room that I had earlier shared with my brother when we had lived there (he, too, had by this time left home), so I knew there was room. That was not the problem. Dad was. He exploded. 'I'm not having no pink-tighted poof in this 'ouse,' he exclaimed, immediately demonstrating his terror of the unknown, and, I suppose, of the danger of running into a homosexual, an encounter he would not have the faintest idea how to deal with. I managed to have my way, but not to involve him. When Graham came to stay, Dad was nowhere to be seen. He would not risk being in the house at the same time, and if he did sleep there, he made sure he was out hours before either of us got up.

Now, of course Graham did not know what my father had said, and there was no way that I would tell him, but with his acute intuitions and long experience of insult, I am quite sure he noticed my father's absence, and knew himself to be the cause of it. He must have been hurt. I would have avoided it if I could, but short of holding my own father in an arm-lock, there was no remedy.

Graham's drinking went completely out of control when his relationship with Petrus came to an end (it may have contributed to this) and when, at the same time, he began to cede precedence to younger men in casting for interesting roles. (David Blair, who had been Margot Fonteyn's regular partner before Rudolf Nureyev dropped from the skies and stole her, also turned to drink, but he was at least happily married.) Living alone in a terraced house near the Hammersmith fly-over, there was nobody to monitor Graham's descent. He began not to turn up for class (an unforgivable lapse in any dancer's routine), and was eventually sent to a clinic to dry out. He came home, but relapsed soon afterwards. He died of alcoholic poisoning at the age of thirty-six. It was a true tragedy, and a warning of the dangers which lurk behind the glamour of public adulation.

The people being applauded are often much more scared and incompetent in life than those of us doing the applauding. We admire the achievement, and neglect the cost.

Paul Clarke died at twenty-five, but it was a terrible accident in vanity which cut him short. He, too, was a magnificent dancer, accomplished in all the leading princely roles, and particularly touching in the adolescent roles of MacMillan's *The Invitation* (wherein he had to be seduced by the older woman, in symmetrical step with his girlfriend's rape by the woman's husband) and *The Two Pigeons*, Ashton's dreamily romantic story of young love lost and won again, which ends, chokingly, with his carrying a live white pigeon on his shoulder in repentance, and another pigeon flying across the stage to join it. Paul, too, was from an unlikely family, his four older brothers all in the building trade and rather dismissive of ballet as a proper career for a bloke. But they were fond of him, and they admired him. He was also every bit as well built as they were, with a honeyed layer of charm which they perhaps lacked. (His lover, however, was Lucette Aldous, the whisky fan mentioned above.)

Apart from a superb physique, Paul also boasted handsome features, with free-flowing blond hair and a dazzling smile. The smile was his undoing. The last time I saw him, he flashed me that famous smile from an open sports car driving through Trafalgar Square. I never understood what he found unsatisfactory about his teeth, which were white, even, and all there. But for some reason he decided to have them 'regularised', as a Hollywood star might, and submitted himself to extensive cosmetic dentistry. Under anaesthetic, poor Paul never woke up. I wept when I heard the news.

While Paul was a dear and intimate friend, another remarkable person who came into my life soon afterwards, or who was, rather, fished in by me, was a man who almost certainly never had a friend in his life, and never wanted one. His long presence in a world of which he was by far the most exotic flower was scattered with a multitude of acquaintances. He discouraged intimacy by a paradoxical readiness to be approached, never refusing an invitation if he could help it, then leaving one with the impression one had encountered a confection, a manifestation of artistic invention in the flesh, not a real person at all. He was also an extraordinary showman, with a name, Quentin Crisp, which was not his own but was among his cleverest tricks. It suggested someone refined, unusual, noble and bizarre. His real name, Dennis Butt, suggested nothing at all.

Quentin's autobiography, *The Naked Civil Servant*, had been turned into a compelling television drama in 1975, with a performance by John Hurt in the title role which rings in the memory still as both an uncanny impersonation and a profound tribute to an unusually brave man. For Quentin had been a flamboyant homosexual, with dyed hair, rouged cheeks, chiffon scarves and provocative mincing gait, at a time in the 1920s and 1930s when such behaviour invited unapologetic violence. Men felt affronted by his very appearance, and attacked him as they might destroy a butterfly which dared to interrupt a boxing-match. He was frequently beaten up, and just as frequently got to his feet, re-ordered his garments, and went on walking, looking, and behaving just as he wished. He was not a rebel. He was an individual.

I suspect it is even a misnomer to call Quentin homosexual, for he had hardly ever had sex with anyone, and was more properly asexual. He once witheringly described the sexual act between men as 'a colostomy without anaesthetic', and was too fastidious to want to invite it. He had even suffered the indignity of being stitched up by the police (a common enough occurrence before the reforms of 1967), who had risibly accused him of importuning them. Quentin found no difficulty in convincing the judge that, looking as he did, it would be unlikely that he could successfully importune anyone with eyes in his head. It was one of the best scenes in the film.

Many of us were riveted by the story and the performance, and found ourselves wondering what sort of man he was. Alastair Londonderry dared me to ask him to dinner at Caithness Road. It was not at all difficult, for there, in the telephone book, was an entry for Quentin Crisp at an address in Beaufort Street, Chelsea. I dialled the number.

At the other end was a voice not so much languid as felinely relaxed. 'Yes?' The word took fully five seconds to pronounce, and the interrogation mark at the end was a quiet challenge. 'I wondered if you would like to come to dinner,' I said, without introduction or explanation. 'Well [another four-second word]', he said, 'as long as nothing better turns up. Where would you like me to go?' The simplicity of the man was tantalising. He did not seek reassurance, did not smell danger, did not worry about motive, merely wanted to know my name and address and what time he should arrive. I did warn him that we should be eight at dinner, but I don't think he cared whether it was two or twelve and a half. He just wanted to oblige.

He was now, I suppose, in his late sixties, and had spent a life trying not to upset or provoke people more than necessary. Since his appearance was itself provocative, and he was not going to change that, in everything else he would do and say whatever was best designed to please, as a kind of emollient. He called everyone Mr and the surname, never using a Christian name as long as I knew him, and did not contradict any proposition that someone made. He was passive appeal personified. When he did express an opinion, it was only because he was asked, not because he ventured it. And then it was worth a dozen vacuous sentences from other more self-important folk. For Quentin was both modest and sharp.

I need not supply examples since he went on to entertain the English-speaking world with one-man shows in which, having presented his monologue, he invited questions from the audience and guaranteed them a polished, sparkling, wise and amusing reply. His prose was as good as Enoch Powell's, and he took as much care as the wily politician in honing it. He might think for a short pause, then out would come a fully-formed sentence, with subject, verb and predicate, subordinate clauses in their proper place, no hesitations or bumps, and a spicy dose of cynicism to lubricate the whole thing. Where one expected syrup from this exaggerated exhibitionist, one received instead three-star pepper, presented all the same with a gentle languor which obviated any bitter taste.

He was able to do this, 'on the wing' as it were, because I am convinced he had been rehearsing his aphorisms all his life. They were the same in my drawing-room as they were on stage. He had perfected the placing of words and their delivery to such an extent that he had something prepared for any eventuality, and they were, in the end, his defence, as effective as a porcupine's quills. For if he could hypnotise people with words, they were less likely to pay attention to his hair or his undulating voice, the very things they found offensive. Language was his armour, and that is why he gave it so much care; his life had occasionally depended upon it.

The end-result was that 'Dennis', whoever he was, had invented somebody who could protect Quentin, and it would work as long as we were never to know who lay behind the polished phrases. It did not matter whether he meant them or not. Nobody would ever know. It did not matter if they reflected his personality or not. Nobody would ever mind. It mattered only that they served their purpose of camouflage and deflection. Quentin Crisp was the most unknowable person I ever met. I visited him at his grotty flat in Beaufort Street, where, it was quite true, the dust had settled for seven years and never got any worse, where every object was dark in hue – dirty brown or black – and where the single bed was turned back like an envelope, into which Quentin glided at night so as to save unnecessary housework. I had lunch with him frequently. I saw him in New York after he had moved to the city of his dreams, where everyone was tolerant (and that also was true), where he lived in another grotty room on 2nd Street on the East Side. But I never knew him. One knows people through their achievements and failures, through their anxieties and distresses, through their desires, expressed or otherwise, and secret shames. One knows them through gossip and shared pleasures, through unexpected moments of anger and long lanes of anguish. And one knows them through laughter. Quentin would open the door to none of these. Even the laughter issued from the neatness of the aphorism, not from the personality of the speaker, which might be anywhere, but was certainly not here, with him, between us. It was an utterly mysterious performance, and hugely clever. And most wondrous of all, despite it one found oneself being very fond of this exotic creature. So perhaps there are threads which bring us to the knowledge of one another without words; those who champion telepathy would enthusiastically concur. I think I mean more than the invisible meeting of thoughts. I mean the unforced shaping of sympathy. One liked Quentin Crisp because he was, in the end, beautiful.

It may seem mischievous, even quixotic, to move from Quentin Crisp to Oswald Mosley, for the two could not be more starkly contrasted. One effete and affected, the other bristling with masculine directness; one contrived and adorned, the other bluntly spare, even somewhat grey, in appearance; the one unexpectedly abstemious and austere (Crisp still, lest you wonder), the other a notoriously self-indulgent philanderer. Of course they never met, moving in worlds so different they might have been from separate species, and they would certainly have detested each other. Yet some surprising qualities connected them despite themselves.

In the first place, both were supremely eloquent. I was too young ever to have heard Mosley in performance, as it were, holding an audience rapt with a wild, impassioned oratory which teetered on the edge of madness, but I did sit for hours in a room in First Street, Knightsbridge, while he, surrounded by a dozen men not themselves noted for their reticence, spoke without interruption or challenge in a flow of persuasive language. I habitually avoid the word 'fascinating', as it denotes mental paralysis and intellectual abnegation, but it is the only word which will do for Mosley in full flood. He did, in fact, fascinate and thereby emasculate his audience; he took their thoughts away from them and replaced them with his own. He intoxicated with his words, until you could not imagine any other words would do, for he gave the impression that only he understood the complexities of international affairs, and that, had he been allowed to deal with them in his way, the world would have been a much saner place. This was oratory indeed, since we all felt, no matter what our political inclinations, that this man was not as sane as he seemed. His intellect was so potent that it overrode his reputation.

Later, I saw him on several occasions in more private circumstances, over lunch at his home near Paris, where again I would be transfixed by his conviction and worldly good sense. It was impossible to contradict him, or to suggest a nuance which might undermine his thesis, not because one was afraid of him in a personal sense, but because one was afraid of his words. One felt intellectually wanting, unable to rise to Mosley's grasp of ideas. This was one of his secrets, the ability temporarily to paralyse the opponent. After every encounter, one left with a frustrating attack of *esprit d'escalier*, rehearsing, too late, all the things one should have said, the points one could have made. Mosley had kidnapped the arena of ideas and made it his own. Everyone else was meant to listen and learn.

This is eloquence of an entirely different order from Quentin's, each of whose polished aphorisms was like a delicately decorated Fabergé egg against Mosley's broad, sweeping El Greco brushstrokes. But it is fair to say they both made language their servant, and used it less as a means of simple communication than a route to control, less as a tool than a weapon, whether defensive (Crisp) or offensive (Mosley).

Then, too, they both had courage, especially in the face of ridicule and overt hostility. Mosley never slunk away to hide from his fierce detractors, but took them frontally and resolved to match their violence with his own. Quentin, in stark contrast, turned the other cheek (often literally), but was no less noble in his resolve not to be cowed. And, in the end, Quentin grew into a national treasure, universally admired and petted, while Mosley never recovered from the contempt into which his Fascist ideology had plunged him.

Which was a pity, since he was a man of considerable charm as well, as is attested, I think, by the fact that his friends called him 'Tom' and his wife called him 'Kit', both diminutives denoting easy affection. Nobody, so far as I know, called him 'Oswald'. In a domestic situation, he was cosy, a home-maker happy with sofas and books and tea, and one could see why Diana adored him. He was a man whom a woman would want to make comfortable, and he would appreciate her efforts. His eyes, hotly piercing in debate, were soft and seductive in repose. I once asked Diana, whom I in turn adored, if she ever minded her husband's terrible philandering (for he was never faithful, and his appetites were rarely sated). She said no, because none of the 'others' mattered, and he always came home to her. It is a hymn sung by many a betrayed wife, and like all truisms, it has its own profound truth. Mosley was never more a man, really, than when he was at home with Diana, not ranting to a crowd, not lusting after a mistress, but quietly at ease with his mate.

Neither Mosley nor his wife ever renounced Fascism, despite the loathsome evidence of its effects. Mosley deplored the diseased promoters of a good idea (Hitler in particular) rather than the idea itself. To the end of his life he believed that he could have made Fascism beneficent. Diana, who continued after his death to attend annual reunions of British fascists in the East End of London, would not traduce his memory by expressing doubts. She was a woman with an enormously kind heart, truly empathetic in a way that I have not encountered in anyone else, yet with that blind spot which would see no wrong in The Idea. When I asked her if she would consider Disraeli to have been an Englishman, she paused for a long time before replying, 'Not really.' Whole books could not have said more, and in that untypically cold response one could see why her sister Jessica continued to distrust her.

Finally, Mosley was never mysterious. Crisp died with his secret intact, nobody ever having known the 'Dennis' concealed within him. Mosley's tragedy was that he had no secrets. Everyone knew what he had done, what he had said, what were his intentions, to the extent that he had no resource of surprise to fall back on. Having no spare card of mystery, he was dismissed by a public who thought they had heard everything. Not that he minded. Mosley was not a man to whine and complain. He had real masculine pride, and I admired him for that.

CHAPTER FOUR

Gentleman's Clubs

The world of the Gentleman's Clubs of London is pregnant with ambience, tradition, weight of years and collective tribal pride. A man's club is more often than not his home, in a way the place where he sleeps and pays his bills can never be. It is where he is himself, fundamentally and without veneer of performance, a place foreign to the habits of dissemblance or approximation. His various selves, as husband, father, professional man, adventurer, are all left outside the door when he ascends the stairs to his club, and there he is quite pure and wiped clean of adjectives and duties, unspecial, unlabelled. And being unspecial, of course, he is also stripped of his titles, honours and privileges, sometimes even of his name (at the Garrick it is considered quite unnecessary to introduce oneself, and I have known friends there for years whose precise identity yet eludes me). He is just another club member, no better and no worse than any other.

In view of all of which, it is no surprise that one's club becomes so essential a part of one's life that it overtakes everything else. There are drawbacks, after all, in marriage and parenthood, even in professional advancement; there can be none in a place where no demands in excess of good nature are made upon you, and the refreshment which this discovery pours upon the new member can be a very dangerous prelude to divorce. It is not unknown for a supposedly neglected wife to consider the club as worse than a mistress.

Being a bachelor, I was luckily free of this danger, and able to embrace club life with the enthusiasm of an adolescent. Which is what I was, in terms of worldly experience, when I was elected to the Garrick at the age of thirty-eight. There are echoes of the boarding-school ethos in every gentleman's club – the long refectory table, the exclusion of women, the louche banter side-by-side with serious philosophical discourse, the nannying by a head waitress reminiscent of Matron, the simple nursery food. But I had not known any of this in the Old Kent Road, at Wilson's Grammar School, or at University College, Cardiff. So club life was not for me, as it patently is for many others, a continuation of boyhood, but an initiation into a new kind of boyhood that had passed me by. It therefore took time for me to learn the ropes, negotiate all those subtly-concealed conventions which public-school men would already have sewn into their veins, and for the first few weeks of my membership, I had to walk up and down Garrick Street for ten minutes or so before plucking up the courage to go in. It did feel a bit like one's first day in long trousers.

It was for this reason, I suspect, that my proposer and seconder did not reveal to me that I was a candidate. They had taken me there three times a year, and I had wondered in awe at the warmth of the walls, and the drapes, and the staircase; the glory of all those theatrical paintings, by de Wilde, by Zoffany; the strange absence of tablecloths (which a Cockney boy would *always* assume indicated High Class, especially if they were damask). It was not, forgive the cliché, for the likes of me. The proportions of the Coffee Room at the Garrick defy description, for they are perfect, as harmonious as a Mozart sonata, and just as comforting. You could not but be happy there. Thus, when I received a letter from the Club Secretary announcing that I had been elected a member at the Committee Meeting the evening before, I immediately assumed a mistake had been made, and telephoned the club to seek elucidation. Gently, it was explained that there was no mistake, and that the Secretary would be pleased to show me round the premises on my first visit as part-owner of them. I know of no other member whose election came to him as a complete surprise, and it was the finest gift I have ever received.

Just as one's friendships vary in kind and in degree, so do clubs differ in their personalities and attractions. I am not competent to speak of White's, Brooks's, Boodles, into each of which I have only ventured as a sometime guest. But I did later become a member of both the Beefsteak and Pratt's, and was able easily to detect the difference in atmosphere. The Garrick is a very special place in terms of its frank bonhomie; indeed this is the one characteristic held against it by its detractors, whether from envy or candid dislike I don't know. I overheard a member of Brooks's complain, 'The trouble with those Garrick people is that they *talk* all the time.' It is true that you do not have to be serious at the Long Table, even if in another life outside the walls you are Chancellor of the Exchequer or Lord Chief Justice. Conversation there is just as likely to be frivolous. At the Beefsteak, on the other hand, if you launch into a subject you are expected to follow it through to a sequential conclusion. It is a little like sitting an examination. If that sounds daunting, it is only because it is bound to be so to me; others may not have a moment's doubt about the apposite nature of their own contribution to the table. I value my time at the Beefsteak, but I cannot pretend I actively *enjoy* it so much as the Garrick. I am always worried that I might put my foot in it. At the Garrick, I often do, and nobody cares.

The Beefsteak has no guest tables, only one elegant long communal table in an oak-panelled room hidden on the second floor of a most unlikely building off Leicester Square. You work your way through sandwich bars, pizza places, shops selling tourist junk, and, until recently, sex shops, to find your way to an anonymous black door leading to a thoroughly different world. Only in England could the juxtaposition occur without causing comment from either side of the divide. The steward who takes your order and the waiter who delivers it are both called 'Charles'. They always have been, whatever their actual names. There have been three 'Charles' in my twenty-five years there, the latest a Swiss who appears to have spent all his adulthood as the Beefsteak 'Charles'. Apart from this, there are two customs which distinguish the club from all others.

The first is the question of who sits at the head of the table, the only seat which sets one apart from every other member present, and which also, of necessity, places one in a position to manage the conversation, or at least gently prod it, on either side. This being to some, I suppose, a seat much coveted, and therefore fought over by people arriving to bag it first, it had been decided long ago that it should be assigned to whomever had been the third person to arrive at the club that morning, a circumstance quite beyond prediction or contrivance. I am sure the reader will anticipate what is coming next. A bundle of nerves when I went to join the party at my new club on the first day, I fell inevitable victim to Sod's Law by being the third to sign in, and found myself presiding over a table which had, on my right, Harold Macmillan, a former Prime Minister, and on my left, Garter King of Arms. I cannot recall a single thing I or they said that day. I only remember longing for the lunch to be over so that I might breathe again.

Incidentally, having said that I am probably the only Garrick member not to have been aware that he was a candidate, I am also probably the only Beefsteak member to have been proposed by two dukes, Their Graces of Devonshire and Portland (though, to be scrupulous about it, Portland was then called Bill Cavendish-Bentinck, inheriting the dukedom afterwards). I am quite sure this sounds like showing off. But as it is a peculiarity above the national average, I think it worth mentioning none the less.

The second Beefsteak custom is the signing-in book, on a table just inside the front-door. At lunch and at dinner, on separate pages, members are expected to sign their names before climbing the stairs to the clubroom itself. Presumably, the historic reason for this curious convention might have been to settle any dispute as to who was the third to arrive, although neither I nor anyone else can imagine any such trivial matter arising. Whatever the origin of the book, its practical effect was to alert you as to who was already in the club before you. And in one notorious case, its effect was more precisely to warn you in time to make your escape.

Every club has its Bore, usually a man whose antennae do not respond to mood and cannot prevent him from saying the wrong thing to the wrong person at absolutely the wrong moment. Or it might be the man who sits eating his meal in silence, answering every jolly enquiry with a snort and a snuffle. (At the Travellers' Club, they long ago gave up trying to correct such people, and instead accommodate them by providing stands on which you can prop a book while eating – behaviour utterly incongruous in a place meant for garrulity.) Or it might be the man who tells you the same story you heard from him on the last occasion. Or, finally, it might be the man whose political views are firm and his need to proselytise even firmer. Club members are uniquely tolerant of their bores, on the very reasonable grounds that, within a year or two, they might well be sufficiently senile to join their number. The only unpardonable sin at the Garrick is to be offensive, or even mildly unkind, to one of the staff. But the Beefsteak boasted the champion bore of the twentieth or any other century, a monumentally charmless creature called Willie Malcolm, who combined in his diminutive frame aspects of all four types of bore mentioned above, and added a spice of meanness all his own.

Willie had been a banker of some sort, and had been born into a wealthy Edwardian family. That was all we knew. His personal life, if there were any, was totally unguessable. He tended to finish a sentence with the meaningless Edwardian coda, 'What! What!', to which there was no possible rejoinder. Since his interlocutors had not been listening very attentively anyway, he was quite happy to proceed as if talking to himself, then shut up suddenly and sink into reverie. So black a blanket did Willie's presence throw over the clubroom, from which there was no escape, there being only one table, and the rules requiring you to be seated in the next vacant chair as the table filled up, that the signing-in book downstairs became a vital blessing. Many were those who, seeing Willie's name on the page in front of them, turned on their heels and left, preferring a plastic table at MacDonald's than another ordeal as his companion.

On one occasion I offered Willie a lift home after dinner. I was driving to Hammersmith, and it would be easy to detour via Victoria to drop him off. He may even have suggested the favour, as a way to save a penny or two on fares. He invited me in before going on. The flat was a marvel of resistance to time, a snapshot of domestic life pre-1914, with veiled lamps, carpets on tables, verdant pot-plants, faded watercolours and dark shadowed wallpaper. Willie told me he had grown up there, and it was blindingly obvious that he had not changed an inch in the décor of his childhood. The flat, though a fascinating archive to an outsider such as myself, to its owner was a metaphor for immaturity. He had preserved the world in which heed had been paid to his words and his wants. He must surely have been a deeply spoilt little wonder, just as he was now a deeply tedious old man. I did not feel sorry for him. I doubt if he lacked contentment. He lived as he wanted to live, alone and aloof.

There was a drinks cabinet against a wall, partly hidden by a sinking armchair, with a glass door through which one could see whisky, port and brandy. He saw that I had noticed it. 'I would offer you a drink,' he said, 'but somehow I have mislaid the key to the cabinet.' I left very shortly afterwards. When he died, it was revealed that he had been a very wealthy man indeed. I had thought it mysterious why he should want to belong to a club at all, until I realised it saved him money. He always chose the cheapest item on the menu, and if that were a tad too pricey, he would ask for omelette and chips.

Having said that club members generally tolerate their bores, I think one may safely make an exception for the Foreign Bore who is not a member but has reciprocal rights to use the club by virtue of his membership of a club overseas, and makes too generous a use of these rights. I was sitting next to the philosopher A. J. ('Freddie') Ayer at the Garrick when we were confronted with an American, who happily ignored me but latched mercilessly on to Freddie. The conversation went something like this:

BORE What do you do?
FREDDIE I don't, I'm retired.
BORE Oh, really? And what did you do?
FREDDIE I taught.
BORE Taught? How interesting. What did you teach?
FREDDIE Philosophy.
BORE Gee, that's great. Where did you teach philosophy?
FREDDIE At Oxford, actually.
BORE Now, where's that?
FREDDIE Oh, do shut up.

Our venerable sage then turned to me and whispered, 'Was I rude?' I could not deny that he had been very peremptory, but he was exonerated by the heroic obtuseness of his interrogator.

The best deflation of pomposity I ever encountered was also at the Garrick, to which I had invited, out of sheer whimsy, a man I did not know, but who happened to bear the same name as myself. He was the Right Reverend Brian Masters, Bishop of Edmonton, whose correspondence I occasionally received in error. I thought it might be fun to meet, and concocted a letter to the effect that 'Mr Brian Masters presents his compliments to the Right Reverend Brian Masters and suggests that the confusion which has arisen as to which of us represents God and which assesses murder ought to be dispelled.' The bishop arrived in his purple, which was already a bad sign, and we dined together at a side-table, talking of not much else but his job, his vocation, his message, and himself. Afterwards I took him Under The Stairs, that cubby-hole with fireplace in the well of the great staircase, to which members habitually repair for port and gossip. There was the redoubtable QC, Caesar James Crespi, vast in girth and reputation, holding forth on one of his pet subjects, the Attorney-General Sir Michael Havers. I introduced my guest, to James's evident chuckling delight. At one glorious moment, lip quivering, pipe waving, James opined, 'Of course, Havers was a shit,' then, spotting my guest's purple, added, 'I'm very sorry to use that word in your presence, Bishop,' to which the purple replied, 'And I'm very sorry to hear it, too.' There was no time for reflection. James returned immediately with, 'Well, I console myself in the knowledge that you're only a suffragan anyway.'

That, too, was rude, but arguably merited. Nobody at the Garrick was allowed to take himself too seriously, even if he was a guest.

There was even an occasion when I was unwittingly rude to David Garrick himself. This, I know, must appear highly fanciful, but no rational explanation for what happened has been forthcoming, so the idea that David was personally offended by what I had done remains imaginatively persuasive.

I had seen in the *Daily Telegraph* reports of the Queen having commissioned the watercolourist Alexander Creswell to execute a series of paintings of the destroyed rooms at Windsor Castle following the disastrous fire of 1992, and that these pictures were now on temporary public exhibition before joining the private royal collection. I went to the exhibition and found myself entranced by Creswell's combination of intense meticulous detail and rare poetic sensibility; he depicted the sadness and hollowness of destruction in a way that a mere recorder could not do, and I learnt that he specialised in interiors, that he had a sense of the personality of rooms and the lyricism of architecture. I also discovered that he was one of the painters who accompanied the Prince of Wales on painting holidays, as a kind of royal tutor; indeed, it was probably Prince Charles who suggested to the Queen that Creswell be given the commission for Windsor. (Many years later, when the rooms had been lovingly restored, Creswell was invited back to do more watercolours – the Before and After comparisons richly enticing to the eye.) From nowhere, it entered my head that I could commission Creswell to do some work for me, a saucy impertinence that even now surprises me. But somehow I have not often been thwarted by timorous hesitation.

The gallery gave me Alexander Creswell's home telephone number, and I told him my plans. He was amazingly ready to oblige, especially as the first subject I suggested was the agonizingly beautiful library at Chatsworth, which I had often visited and gawped at, wherein I had once done some work, and where several times in winter the fire had been lit, a table had been laid, and dinner had been served to Andrew, Debo and myself in a strangely cosy atmosphere amid perfect eighteenth-century warm-wooded book-infested splendour. He was very keen on this, and the people at Chatsworth were helpful, as always, in giving him access. The painting which emerged is a glorious affirmation of one of England's most beautiful rooms. It now hangs on my wall in France.

Given that I adored the Coffee Room at the Garrick with something like infatuated madness, I wondered whether Alexander could capture this love on canvas, through a careful depiction of the colours and proportions which made the room so seductive. He was, again, very willing to take on the commission, and I very excited at the prospect. For good measure, I also asked for a second painting, of the grand staircase which offers such an embrace as one enters from the street. This turned out to be a trifle too cheeky, and I was to receive reproach from a most unexpected quarter.

The paintings were duly delivered, and they too now hang here in France. But I conceived the notion that for a few months before being shipped, they should be left on view at the club for other members to enjoy, and so we arranged for two easels to be placed on the first-floor landing, outside the bar, and beside the banisters at the top of the grand staircase (there was, of course, no wall-space anywhere, with thousands of things already on show). Here the paintings were displayed, and much admired, save for a calamity which occurred after the first three weeks.

The Club Secretary called me one Monday morning to announce that one of the pictures had been found smashed at the foot of the staircase, having ostensibly collapsed and fallen from the landing. It had been left safely in place when the club had closed the previous Friday, and nobody had been on the premises from that time until opening on Monday morning, when the smashed remains were found. Everyone was worried and apologetic, but more than that, mystified. I went round to see. The frame could be repaired or replaced easily enough, and having told Alexander what had happened, I was assured that any touching-up could be achieved in such a way that one would never know any damage had occurred. But how on earth did the picture get to be at the bottom of the stairs in the first place, without any human agency?

A careful examination of the landing revealed that the picture could not have simply fallen. The easel was still in place, and the bannister was some eighteen inches higher than the pegs of the easel on which the picture rested. The pegs, too, were still in place. Had the painting slid from its secure position, it would have fallen *down*, and therefore been found at the bottom of the easel, on the landing itself. To be instead at the bottom of the stairs, it would have had to lift itself *upwards* and hurl itself *over* the bannister, a feat patently impossible for an object to achieve. Yet there was nobody in the building.

The picture of the Coffee Room was untouched. It was the picture of the staircase that had suffered this ignominious insult. Why? All photographs of the staircase show it from below, as it sweeps up to the half-landing before turning to the left and on up towards the first floor. In the corner of that half-landing, beneath the portrait of Nell Gwynn, sits David Garrick's own chair, one of the most precious objects in the building, and certainly one of the most emotionally-charged. With its elegant arms, its worn red damask upholstery, it speaks of David's own presence in the house named after him. But Alexander had elected not to paint the staircase from that viewpoint. He wanted his picture to contain the entrance as well, with daylight coming in from the street and from the domed ceiling high above, so that the sweep of the staircase from below as well as soaring up above to the landing and the bar could be contained within the one frame. It was a bold idea, but it had, of course, one casualty. The only way he could attain this view was by standing in the corner where David's chair sat, which meant, inevitably, that the one object that was missing from his picture was the chair itself. David, apparently, was miffed.

The driver of the van which came to collect the picture was in no doubt. ' 'E's been at it again, 'as 'e?' he said. 'It's not the first time I've 'ad to clear up after that ghost. 'E's very sensitive, y'know.' It was the first time I had ever heard of a Garrick ghost, and I have never heard him mentioned since. Perhaps he is an embarrassing secret. I had to conclude that David himself, irritated at his exclusion from his own abode, had thrown my picture to the floor. It may not be much of an explanation for those readers who cling to their sanity, but it is the only one I have. I now pause to acknowledge the chair, with abject apology and respect, every time I pass it.

Two more clubs complete my tally, though one of them, Aspinall's, is not a gentleman's club in the traditional sense. The third of John Aspinall's famous gambling casinos (the first was the Claremont in Berkeley Square, setting the standard as soon as new gaming laws in 1962 made such places permissible for the first time in two hundred years), it occupies premises in Curzon Street, which is nifty to say the least, considering Aspers' wife was Lady Sarah Curzon. Sumptuously furnished and decorated with a self-conscious, even declamatory lavishness, which stops just short of being vulgar (the vulgarity preciously claimed by some of the members), Aspinall's is warm in its welcome, discreet in its encouragement. For it is, ultimately, a place designed to separate witless gamblers from their huge booty, and this must be done with a mixture of flattery and enticement. The flattery is in the décor, which makes them feel they deserve such trappings, and the enticement in the other members, in whose presence the gambler does not wish to be seen as cautious, shifty, or cowardly. The atmosphere is subdued, respectful, slightly secretive or furtive, as if we were somewhere we should not be and must keep our voices down so as not to attract attention. It is all part of the wonderfully choreographed daily opera which

Aspers contrived to 'give gamblers a good name', and it worked so well that his casino became the standard against which all others were measured. It also afforded him the more than £2 million a year he needed to house and feed the rare animals he had rescued from extinction, and was breeding for dispersal back into the wild – again a pioneering endeavour which has since been copied the world over.

Aspers made me an honorary family member, with the right to dine at the club free of charge, as a reward for my 1988 biography of him, which was the first printed account to take his work seriously. Acting against character, I tried not to over-do the privilege, and tended to dine there only three or four times a year, more often than not alone. I only once went upstairs to the gaming-rooms, to taste a flavour of the place. Otherwise I remained grounded, with a lavish menu of English, Chinese and Middle-Eastern dishes, and the best wine-list I knew anywhere; it was the only place I dared to order a Château La Lagune or, even better on one occasion, a Château Petrus. The few seconds of guilt which blushed my cheeks were dis-pelled by a quick reflection upon the hundreds of thousands of pounds being taken just above me, on the next floor, during the time it took to enjoy just one glass.

The other club which was a treat, to which I was not elected or required to pay dues, could not have been more different. This was Pratt's, a tiny establishment in the basement of a terraced house off St James's Street, founded in the eighteenth century and now belonging to the Duke of Devonshire. As such, it has its committees, its trustees, its candidates and presum-ably its blackballs, but ultimately the owner can override all these and nominate whomever he wants as one of his personal members. Thus it was that, after dinner at Chatsworth in 1976, Andrew suddenly asked me, out of the blue, if I should like to become a member of Pratt's. I had never given the matter a thought, but the honour was so exhilarating, and the gift so utterly unforeseen, that I accepted immediately. 'I should warn you,' he said, 'that it is a jolly place for geriatrics. You will enjoy it in the end.'

There is one table in a small dining-room, which could easily be in somebody's house (in fact it is, I suppose, for the building has not been tampered with, save to add a lavatory off the billiard-room with two urinals side-by-side, which would not be found in any of my neighbours' houses). The table can seat about fourteen. Next door, where we sit for drinks beforehand and coffee afterwards, in front of an original coal-fired stove, is the drawing-room. It is all delightfully cosy, and extremely private. While at the Beefsteak all the servants are called Charles, at Pratt's they are all called George, and when a lady was appointed to be the new George, we christened her Georgiana in honour of the fabled Duchess of Devonshire of the eighteenth-century, whose biography I had also written (it was the first, by the way, to draw upon original letters and documents. Miss Foreman's political and amazingly successful account came twenty years later). The food is relentlessly breakfast-style, with all types of eggs, accompanied by sausages and bacon and tomatoes and mushrooms, but nothing exotic. Considering that it is produced from a cubby-hole off the drawing-room, it is miraculous that it should be so good, even if limited.

I soon saw what Andrew meant by his warning. The place is replete with retired politicians and landowners from distant parts who still regard London as a den of vice. They all have acres and all shoot grouse. One of them, feeling that he should make some enquiry of me as he had not seen me before, asked me what about some farming matter, it being assumed, of course, that this was the one common subject upon which any gentleman would be adequately informed, to ease conversation; it was, in other words, an ice-breaker. I, naturally, had not the faintest idea what he was talking about. So he, befuddled, was obliged to pursue his enquiries further. When I told him I was a writer, he looked in frightened astonishment, as if he had never encountered such a creature before. 'What?' he exclaimed, 'a writer-chappie? You mean . . . books?' He had obviously only seen such objects on shelves, and imagined they were placed there by his ancestor's decorator.

Talking of the side-by-side *pissoirs* at Pratt's reminds me of a Garrick story, which is often ascribed to the actor-manager Sir Seymour Hicks, although these stories can switch ownership quite easily without losing their spice, or indeed their original veracity. The Garrick used to have Victorian lavatories, with precisely the great marble dividing slabs which still exist at Pratt's, although rather more of them. A committee meeting in the 1950s elected to throw out these rather elegant monstrosities and replace them with more modern eye-level (as it were) contraptions then becoming fashionable in public urinals. Sir Seymour objected and voted against the innovation, but it was none the less carried by a majority and he had to acquiesce, grumbling the while.

On the day the new lavatory was opened for use, Sir Seymour was seen to exit therefrom. Another member accosted him. 'Ah, Seymour,' he said, 'I see you've used the new loos. What do yer think of 'em, eh?' 'Very fine, very clean, very posh,' came the measured reply. 'Trouble is, they make my cock look a bit shabby.'

That is not, as it happens, a tale you might hear in any club. Most of them are more decorous with their humour than is the Garrick. But at least Garrick stories are true; they are not 'tall', nor are they apocryphal, and their humour, if a little bawdy, has the uncommon knack of loosening even those tight-lipped frozen faces which a lifetime of proper behaviour has protected from every rude word. My favourite is so unlikely that it has to be preceded by the promise of its absolute truth. This happened. It happened in an English courtroom. And it happened to a man whom I knew very well, my closest friend at the Garrick – the rotund Crespi already mentioned above for having deflated my namesake.

James was a famous prosecutor. I asked him once if he had ever defended. 'Oh yes,' he said, 'when I was young. I had to, you know. You took whatever came your way. In fact, one of my very first cases was in defence of a clergyman, arrested in a public lavatory in Lancing. It appears this lavatory was famous the world over – people came from Port Said to visit it – by reason of a loose brick between two cubicles. Gentlemen used regularly to avail themselves of the opportunities which this loose brick presented. What none of them knew was that there was also a hole in the ceiling, and the local police officers used to park themselves on the roof, with their cucumber sandwiches, the better to observe what was going on. Occasionally they would drop down and arrest gentlemen in their droves. One of those arrested was my poor clergyman. So, when the arresting officer came into the witness-box to give his evidence, I thought it might put him at his ease if I commiserated with him. I said, "It must have been a very unpleasant duty, officer." Do you know what he replied? He said, "Yes, sir. To tell you the truth, sir, when somebody came in for a good honest shit, it was like a breath of fresh air." '

Now that is not something one can make up.

One other inspired defence that James came up with also concerned lavatory behaviour. (This is not to imply that such offences were a national epidemic, only that the few which did come before the courts tended to be remembered by those involved for their uncommon spiciness, and barristers are notoriously unshockable anyway.) A man was arrested for whispering lewd suggestions through the wall of a cubicle. In the neighbouring cubicle was a police officer, who promptly knocked on the door and arrested the whisperer. James asked the policeman if he had looked at the walls of the cubicle.

'No, sir.'

'Then you did not notice if anything was written on them?'

'No, sir.'

'Thank you, officer. No further questions.'

The defendant was called to give evidence, and James put to him the very same question, as to whether he had glanced at the walls. He said he had done so.

'And did you notice anything about the walls?'

'Yes, I did.'

'And what was that?'

'They were covered with graffiti.'

'And could you make out what they said?'

'Yes. In fact, I was so astonished, I even read them out to myself.'

After which, the charges were dropped.

I have written with spirit, admiration and love of James Crespi in another book. He was utterly unique, and it is true he was very much at home in his club. But was he a 'typical' club member? I think probably not quite, and not just because of the three stories here recorded. He did not subordinate himself to the club. His life was not a daily preparation for his evening there, for he adored his professional life at the Bar, and loved the law above all things. It oiled his mind, tightened his grammar, stimulated his moral sense, and gave daily proof of the nobility of justice properly administered. I never heard anyone defend the jury system so eloquently as he, and he would roundly and roughly turn upon anyone who suggested it was flawed, or that juries could not be trusted to reach the right conclusion. For James, the club was relaxation following the stress and concentration of dealing with villains. But for some, club-life risked ballooning into the very purpose of existence.

The man who most exemplified this characteristic, and who must therefore be regarded as the 'typical' clubman, was Sir Iain Moncreiffe of that Ilk ('of that Ilk' means, I believe, 'of the same name', because his full appellation was Iain Moncreiffe of Moncreiffe). He could not have been more unlike James Crespi, rotund of girth and of phrase. Iain was slim, patrician, polite, slightly remote, full of good stories yet none of them as wicked as those above; in fact, it says much of his personality that I would never have dared repeat them to him. There was something of the *précepteur* about him, a man destined to teach and to guide, a man without doubts, but only because he knew what he was talking about, not because he was boastful or arrogant in any way; on the contrary, Iain was, if not modest, at least careful not to display his knowledge, as if to do so would be to take unfair advantage of somebody who knew less than he. Cautious diffidence was a habit of breeding, but his knowledge was encyclopaedic, and I use the word with great purpose, for he did indeed carry within his head a veritable encyclopaedia of aristocratic history.

I knew him first at the Beefsteak, but that was just one of his many clubs. I forget how many he belonged to, and it was a constant wonder to many that he could visit five of them in one evening, with tea at one, drinks at another, dinner at a third, port at a fourth, and a night-cap for good measure at the last. We came together in the first place because I was researching for my book *The Dukes*, and quite fortuitously mentioned this as we dined. Little did I then know that Iain Moncreiffe was a richer source of research in his own person that all twenty-four volumes of *The Complete Peerage*, plus *Burke's* thrown in for additional tit-bits. I suppose that cannot *literally* be true, and I should not spoil what is already an astonishing achievement by needless exaggeration. But many were our conversations in which he would, from memory, retrace the antecedents, on both sides, up to the eighth generation, of any royal or aristocratic house in Europe. This involved an exercise of memory which brought in hundreds of individuals, often over and over again, as different tracks brought back into view a line which had wandered off into the darkness shortly before. Not only this, but his knowledge of African tribal ancestry seemed to be just as extensive, with the result that he left one reeling with factual and genealogical concussion. I think he even once demonstrated to me how Queen Elizabeth II was descended from Dracula.

There was quite simply no one in the country who could match Iain Moncreiffe for family data. And since he was himself related to every noble house in Europe, in some way or other, the exercise was no mere historical romp, but an analysis of self as well. In a funny way, his excessive knowledge of his own and everyone else's ancestry demonstrated, in the way that paradox does, just how ordinary aristocratic families finally are, for every one of us has just as many hundreds of ancestors as did Iain, save that we cannot name them. I think this unexpected fruit of his knowledge secretly delighted him.

Excessive in his memberships, in his genealogy, Iain was also excessive in his capacity for drink. It would traduce his memory to dwell upon this in order to titillate, still worse to denigrate, but with Iain Moncreiffe neither motive would ever suggest itself. His drunkenness was simply spectacular, heroic, to be celebrated more than chastised. I would go and stay with him at the ancestral home in Perthshire, called Easter Moncreiffe, where he would warn me that the only essential dress was a pair of bedroom slippers, for we did not intend to go out much, but would sit and talk for hours. And drink. Several drinks preceded lunch. More than one bottle accompanied it. Liqueur of more than one ilk would follow. And it was not unusual for me to help his wife lug the inert, and by now affectionately talkative, body of Iain up the stairs to bed. She could not have done the job alone, for he was now heavy with relaxation of limb, and I would put my hands under his armpits and pull him up, one stair at a time. I never asked, but I suppose when Lady Moncreiffe had no visitors she would have to leave him slumped and snoozing in the dining-room. By six o'clock he was awake and eager to continue the conversation (about the Hohenzollerns, or the split dukedoms of Hamilton and Abercorn, or Churchill's maternal forebears) where we had left off. Ready also for the first gin-and-tonic of the evening.

He was in himself the best of all tonics. And being a clubman to his fingertips, as well as a romantic with unerring radar to detect the proximity of a beautiful woman, he was implacable in his hostility to the notion that the gentleman's clubs should 'move with the times' and open their doors to female membership. A few clubs have already given in, the Reform in Pall Mall being the most notable, but the majority find the idea not exactly distasteful, but downright foolish. Occasionally a small cabal of members at the Garrick opens up the suggestion to an Annual General Meeting, and the matter has to be put to the vote. The ensuing debate engenders such passion that the meeting has to take place outside the club premises, since virtually every member is likely to turn up, including those few hundred who show their faces less than once a year. The last time this occurred, we met at the old Royalty Theatre off Kingsway, and there was not a spare seat in the auditorium. Rational and sensible speeches were made in support of the proposal for women members, but the vote went overwhelmingly against, by about ninety-five per cent. As I was one of those to resist the innovation, it might serve well for me to justify my vote in these pages.

It is alone interesting that I feel it necessary to use the word 'justify'. It comes naturally. That can only be because I feel, somewhere, that the exclusion of ladies is a ridiculous anachronism which cannot be explained, can only be felt. One may explain something which is motored by factual considerations and sequential logic, but one can only place before the reader a conviction that relies upon unprovable certainties of heart. Hence the need for 'justification'. I cannot demonstrate why ladies should not be members of my club, but I can tell you how a decision to admit them would render me desolate. That day would rob me of my club and substitute for it another institution which I did not join. To take the Garrick, yet again, as an example. It is what it is, and its members are men. There is no question of rightness or wrong-ness in this (although one could debate for hours why it should be that men like to be together and feel comfortably protected from the presence of women, a pretty deep matter to digest). Lady members would transform the place into something else. Its degree of relaxation, its openness of conversation, its sub-terranean current of affections, would all be compromised, and in their place one might find stiff self-conscious politeness, self-censorship, elegant flirtations. These are all splendid things in themselves, and I have welcomed them at dinner-parties in my own home, as well as at weekends in the houses of others. But one does not go to one's club to have them there repeated. One goes for a different kind of company.

Shortly after I was elected to the Garrick, a new club in Soho was founded, called Groucho's. From the beginning, it was open to both men and women, and so, from the beginning, it has been a friendly and agreeable private restaurant. It has never become a club. Those who want a private restaurant could hardly do better than join Groucho's, where, by the way, lots of deals are made, influence is sought and promised, and the process called 'networking' can be observed like a meccano-set in action. Those who prefer a club might hope for election to Brooks's, White's, Pratt's, or the Garrick, where deals are forbidden and 'networking' is unheard of. It is largely because women do not believe this last assertion that the subject crops up every few years.

For twenty-seven years I have looked forward to the occasions when I can take a lady guest to the Garrick for dinner at a side-table. Without exception, they tell me it is a treat far more valuable than had it been a right. Natalia Makarova comes with me there every time she is in London, and she is well aware that her exotic appearance adds a flash of glamour to the room, so she takes pains to look more flamboyant with each visit. Beryl Bainbridge on the other hand, fairly indifferent to glamour, enjoys the cerebral tingle of the place, and dines there with me, instead of at the corner bacon-and-eggs café which she favours, for a 'night out'. Elizabeth Cavendish takes it for what it is; it would never enter her mind to question its *raison d'être*, having all her life been a woman of achievement in a man's world, her father and brother dukes, herself a mere daughter. And my own Camilla, also a daughter who, had she been born male, would herself be Duke, relishes the Garrick for its gallantry and attention to the ladies who adorn it as guests. None of these people would dream of lobbying for the club to change its nature and its tone. They want it as it is.

There are two ladies I think of as almost honorary members, because they are frequently taken there and are always happy to be 'home'. One is Betty Boothroyd, former Speaker of the House of Commons, who goes as the guest of Murdo McLean, former head of the Whips' Office. And the other is Judi Dench, whose late husband Michael Williams was elected on the same day as myself in 1977. So Judi has known the club for as long as I have. And an extra layer has been added to her friendship by the warm sadness of Michael's death at a time when both he and I were in hospital.

I have already told in *Getting Personal* of Michael's after-dinner speech when he and Judi were Guests of Honour at a special occasion there. Here I may perhaps elaborate on my long connection with them.

Along with everyone else, I was first seduced by Judi's voice. My old friend Elio Nissim, a Florentine lawyer who had settled in England and become rhapsodically English in habits and manner, with a collection of over two hundred rare British walking-sticks, asked me to bring her down for tea at his secluded cottage in Cookham, Berkshire. Elio had been head of the Italian division of the BBC World Service during the Second World War and had maintained his connections there. I think he had had cause to interview Judi for the Italian radio, and had been captivated by her. He and his wife Angela longed to entertain her in the proper English manner, with tea and scones and tiny sandwiches.

Judi was then in the first flush of her fame. She had left the Central School of Drama and gone straight to the Old Vic to play Ophelia to John Neville's Hamlet. A number of prime classical roles tumbled into her lap and she was already lauded, in her early twenties, as the finest Shakespearean actress of the day. She had been in Chekhov's *Cherry Orchard* with a line-up of other notables including Peggy Ashcroft and John Gielgud and had been noted more than any of them. Then she had stunned everyone by being cast as the first English Sally Bowles in the musical *Cabaret* at the Cambridge Theatre (years before Liza Minelli made a memorable film version). She was the one person in the theatre everyone was talking about. And this was the lady I was supposed to take to tea in Cookham.

I telephoned her out of the blue and made my proposal. She was not shocked, not determined to refuse, but quite sensibly said, 'Wouldn't it be a good idea if we were to meet first?' And in *that voice*. She could ask any man to waltz with a hippopotamus and he would do his best to oblige. The voice was the aural equivalent of the best honey-coated Belgian champagne chocolate truffle, and each sentence she uttered was yet another truffle from what was evidently an inexhaustible box. She was music, from the lower, sensuous second-violins. She was a scented bower. She was a lush mature Burgundy. And all this simply from a voice, which was sometimes quite inadequately described as 'husky'. In an earlier generation, Joan Greenwood had a similar instrument, which you can hear to the full in the early film version of *The Importance of Being Earnest*. But Greenwood managed it, slid it around her lips, skilfully played with it as, in a different way, Marilyn Monroe would later. But Judi Dench's voice just was what it was, without artifice or development.

She well knew that her voice was unusual, though she would prefer to call it bizarre rather than beautiful. For an actor, she was always paradoxically unwilling to show off. I once saw her place a notice on the board outside the Royal Shakespeare Theatre in Stratford-upon-Avon which announced, *Miss Dench does not have a cold. She always sounds like that.*

We dined at a small Italian restaurant called La Campanella in Romilly Street, behind the theatre. It is still there. We giggled a lot, for Judi longs for laughter and truth, in equal measure, the one frivolous desire tempering the other deeply serious one. On stage, only the truth matters, and she must be the medium for its revelation to an audience. Off stage, she wants nothing more than to roar with pleasure at the ridiculous and the un-expected. This is not to suggest that she is lightweight; in a solemn and important personal conversation she can be heart-warmingly receptive, listening hard, trying to understand, making sure she has some sympathetic or helpful contribution to make. But she still best enjoys a laugh, or a long-winded game with pen and paper in a company of six; the one naturally leads to the other.

We made a date to motor out to Cookham. It was a pleasant tea, and everyone was happy. She gently pointed out that she relied upon me to make sure we got back to London in time for her performance in *Cabaret*. The curtain was due to go up at 7.30, and actors had to be on the premises in good time for the 'half', when a check is made at 6.55 p.m. that everyone has arrived and is in their dressing-rooms. If anyone is missing, the understudy is told to get himself or herself ready to take over. I of course undertook to ensure safe and early arrival. The journey to London was only half an hour, and allowing for another half-hour to make one's way through to the centre of town, there would be no serious difficulty.

On the motorway we encountered a totally unjustified and hideously severe traffic-jam. We inched forward every few seconds, and stopped again. It was obviously a nightmarish situation, for there was no alternative but to drive on and trust to the stars. Judi tried hard not to convey her anxiety to me, for she is among the most considerate of people I have ever met, but there was no denying that she was worried, nor that I was scared. I chattered on to smother the apprehension. She, uncharacteristically, was dead quiet.

I think we arrived at 7.15 p.m., technically too late, and very awkward for her who had to make-up at speed, when any actor likes to have time to prepare. Indeed, the understudy may already have been confirmed in the part by then. I have the dimmest memory that for some reason there *was* no understudy, and that Judi simply *had* to be there, but I cannot verify this, because I have never had the courage to ask her. I was sunk in shame and embarrassment, and should have despised myself if indeed she had missed the performance. So I preferred not to know. Perhaps if she reads this she will tell me, more than forty years later.*

It says much for Judi's steadfastness that not once did her behaviour towards me reflect that I had once seriously let her down. For all I know, she may well have joked about it. I was very pleased when she and Michael Williams decided to marry, for they had both suffered unhappy misjudgements in flirtation, Michael with a woman who was among my closest friends. He was probably even more steady than she was, his feet firm to the ground, his dedication to his profession taking second-place to his tenacity when faced with the trials of reality. When there was trouble, he would disappear to the pub for a pint, secure in the company of ordinary folk who had no truck with stage pretensions. Judi, on the other hand, counted mainly theatricals among her friends, but could rely on her splendid mother, who I fancy talked sense to her all the time.

The wedding took place at St Mary's, Hampstead, in the centre of the London village and a short walk from Judi's little house overlooking the old church cemetery. She is a Quaker. Michael was a Catholic. They both held dear to their faith. So the ceremony embraced both. But the most extraordinary circumstance derived from the role that Judi was playing at Stratford at the time. In *The Winter's Tale*, two of the parts are mother and daughter, Hermione and Perdita. They share a scene in the last act, when the daughter, having long been missing, is reunited with her mother. Judi Dench broke with custom by playing both roles herself, helped by some imaginative and clever stage-management in that final scene. Only one actress before had ever attempted such a trick, and that was Mary Robinson in about 1902. And Mary Robinson was married in the same church in Hampstead. The reception took

---

* Happily, she confirms that she made it.

118

place at London Zoo. I have no information as to where Mary Robinson's wedding-party was celebrated.

When my biography of E. F. Benson was published in 1991, Judi and Michael handsomely came to the local bookshop in Hampstead to give readings. No agents were involved, and it would never occur to them to expect a fee. Ease of favours in the entertainment world are comparatively rare, but I know that both Judi and Michael would consider a favour more precious than a contract.

Another of her special qualities is honesty, reflected both in her performances (her portrayal of Lady Macbeth being so true to the sense of evil that it made her ill) and in her frequently hilarious stories. I say this not to flatter, but to alert the reader, yet again, that he must push his natural scepticism aside. One of Judi's earliest roles was Juliet at the Old Vic, for which she received much praise. She decided to celebrate her success by bringing her parents down from York, quite an undertaking for people not used to travel far. She organised the train, the hotel, and the tickets, dead-centre, in Row E of the stalls. Could not be better. At one moment in the play, Juliet, bereft and forlorn in her acute misery, is alone with her nurse, and has the passingly important line, 'Nurse, oh nurse, where is my father?' Whereupon Dr Dench promptly stood up in the stalls and addressed the stage with, 'Here we are, Judi, in Row E.'

Judi tells the story, so it must be true.

CHAPTER FIVE

Dealing with Children

Part of my professional life has been devoted to attempting to make sense of some of the most distressing acts of wickedness of which men are capable, a task which has brought upon me some ill-conceived opprobrium. There are common assumptions: (a) that to comprehend is to condone, forgive, even encourage acts of deep injury to others, such as murder and torture, which is why I consciously avoid the verb *understand*, with its undercurrent of sympathy; and (b) that to pay attention to the motives and psychological triggers of aberrant conduct is to be utterly indifferent to the victims of that conduct. A moment's thought on either of these propositions would reveal their fatuity, but critics on this level are not keen on thought, with its detours into ambiguity. They prefer the certainty of emotional conviction, of which the worst of our tabloid newspapers provide them an abundant supply. In addition, of course, the ferocity of their indignation against writers like myself who dissect such subjects suggests they are drawn to these subjects by a powerful attraction which drenches them in guilt. The newspapers which revel in these matters sell millions of copies; my books, which try to take a closer analytic look, do not.

There is, however, one wickedness which I have scrupulously avoided writing about. On the vexed matter of sexual abuse of minors, or child molestation, or pederasty, I cannot be sure that any investigation that I might make would be free of bias, uncontaminated by special pleading. Or, at least, I could not wholly blame those people who might suggest that it was. I should not only have to be exceptionally clear in my own mind where I stood on the issue, and think about it with intensity and application, but I should need superlative powers of persuasion in words to carry my readers with me, and these I doubted I would be able to summon. But this stuff ought to be addressed some time, and honesty remains the only worthwhile tool with which to address it. So now might be the time, and I shall see to what conclusions my meanderings might lead.

In the first place, it is a tremendous relief to be able to start with one overwhelming truth. I am stunned into bewildered horror by the stories I hear of the sexual exploitation of infants. Until recently, I had no idea that such a thing was possible, but with the spread of Internet availability, it appears that hundreds of thousands of people routinely watch images of very young children being subjected to humiliation at the hands of adults who, in a sane world, should be there to provide them with the protection they quite rightly expect. One investigation showed that any individual man might have ten thousand of these pictures (more than he would ever have time to look at, one might think), and that the men who spend their leisure hours collecting and cataloguing these images can be stockbrokers, greengrocers, policemen, anyone at all. Just as the Germans who kept the Nazi concentration camps running smoothly while people were degraded before their very eyes were ordinary chaps with wives and children, pets and hobbies, so the collectors of child pornography appear, for the most part, to lead unobjectionable lives. In the case of the Nazis, it was because they were given the sanction of law and the authority of the State to do what they did, and they were moreover taught that the wretches whose lives were thus gradually stolen from them were not really human anyway.

But those who enjoy child pornography have no such excuse (if excuse it be). There is no quasi-lawful organisation to support them, no folk-mythology to encourage them, yet they exist in great numbers. Why?

A television programme showed a few of these images in order to tell the viewer exactly what they were talking about. Of course, great slabs of the pictures were blacked out, but enough remained visible for it to be apparent what was going on, and that sexual gratification of the adult was the only purpose detectable. I can quite believe Jack Straw who, when as Home Secretary he had to see some of this material, revealed quite clearly that he was physically nauseated by it. So, if it is repellent, why are some people, a lot of people, not repelled by it? Or are they repelled, and do they enjoy the sensation of self-disgust which they wrap around themselves? Why do some find it more exciting to inflict sexual activity upon an individual too young to know what that activity is for, let alone willingly to participate in it? These are fearfully difficult questions to answer, for they are very awkward ones to reflect upon. Which means that one's thoughts might be diverted by all those intrusive elements of indignation and self-protection which I enumerated earlier, and which I have always tried to avoid. It needs a very clear head indeed.

It is frequently stated that what is most precious about children is their innocence, and that it is this which is corrupted by adult sexual attentions. Well, innocence means the state of not-being-harmful, and I am not sure it is good enough in the context. After all, little boys and little girls can be very harmful indeed, towards one another and towards animals. They also have an imperfectly formed notion of their sexual abilities, and are not slow to investigate them. No, I think the use of the word 'innocence' here gives away what the user of the word would *like* the problem to be about, and that is sexual conquest. Most men prefer a virgin, and would welcome the chance to initiate her. It is an integral part of the purpose of sexual conquest to be the first to impregnate and ensure the proliferation of one's genes. So, when one talks of the 'innocence' of children who are sexually tampered with, one is surreptitiously indicating that, while powerfully condemning the acts themselves, one understands their attraction. This is deeply dangerous, because wholly unconscious. The enemies of child pornography unwittingly demonstrate that they know why it is there, and further, that they *feel* the possibility of the pleasure which they condemn.

No, a much better word is the *purity* of the young. They do not have to be totally harmless or totally new, but their essence lies in the purity of their mischief. It is absolutely in the nature of childhood to be unsullied by the multiple resonances which beset whatever an adult says or does. The slow emergence from this state into adolescence and then maturity is, as all the poets have noted, the sadness of a childhood left behind. What the pornographers do, then, is to insult childhood itself, to pour sewage into spring water, to attack the preciousness of pre-experience. It is, in absolute terms, a *spiritual* crime, and the faces of the infant victims of these incomprehensible (to them) assaults reveal not disgust, but spiritual death. They can recover from other aspects of their ordeal, but not from this.

One might therefore look to a corruption of the spiritual impulse for a possible explanation of this deviance. It is curious, for example, that just as no other species, so far as we can tell, is capable of investing life with a spiritual dimension, so too no other species indulges in the abuse of its young ones. I certainly have never come across a scientific paper of any sort which suggested that sexual interference with minors was a characteristic of any other group of mammals. In this, as in so much else, we are apparently unique. It might seem, then, that to impose adult sexual activity upon infants, to toxify them, to de-purify them, is subconsciously to resist that spiritual pull which should ennoble all of us. It is as if the demands of spiritual life, the possibilities of rapture and bliss, the requirements to sublimate and concentrate attention upon the non-material and non-physical, are too much for some people, who therefore feel wanting and insufficient, and visit their frustration upon the purity of childhood in a kind of defiant revenge. By transforming children into objects of their lust, and in dislocating their identity as beings to be cherished, the abusers are staking their right to an utterly selfish non-spiritual life, having found themselves unable to reach those higher levels of humanity which they intuit are around them. Their abuse is a manifestation of scorn and contempt and inadequacy, and I think it is no accident that sexual attacks upon children, especially that arid, empty, emotionless, functional sort which finds its way into pornographic images, is widespread in countries with Western religions, wherein spirituality should be an obligation.

It is no paradox that children are sometimes defiled by Christians, and universally revered by Buddhists. The spiritual maturity of Buddhists lies in seeing the spirit in every living thing, all around one all the time, so much so that it is taken for granted as integral to life, whereas in the Western religions it is something that has to be striven for, inculcated, sought after, a doctrine that presupposes some will succeed in the quest and others will not. Failure is written into the text, and failure produces resentment. Priests and clerics who do not live up to their own spiritual expectations (and I have personally watched some sweating with the struggle) are more likely to collapse into the self-disgust of child-abuse than those who are spiritually calm. Buddhists are calm. You do not see children used as sex-objects in the Far East, except by visiting Westerners.

All this is deeply difficult to prove, because it is a matter for philosophical speculation, not scientific demonstration. It may be true; it may not. Less nebulous, perhaps, are those explanations which are rooted in empirical observation, and which have found voice in the imaginations of poets through the ages. The empirical agenda was made common currency by the twentieth-century embrace of popular psychiatry, especially that of Freud and Adler. And this suggests that a fundamental fear in any sexual approach is the fear of refusal. There appears to be no more bitter hurt felt by a man than to have his sexual gifts discounted, diminished, or disprized.

Of course, one may attempt persuasion to overcome resistance, and in this joyful and enticing exercise lies the whole point of a sexual approach in the first place. This gradual slipping of the individual desire into a reciprocal shared encounter is what sexual love is all about, and that is why the pursuit and the persuasion have always been the stuff of romance. But if one lacks the confidence to take on the task, and the first refusal is seen not as a disguised inducement but as an outright rejection, then the wounded suitor retreats into solitariness and must find other ways to satisfy his needs *without* the danger inherent in reciprocity. The simplest method is fantasy, imagining the encounter which has not happened, and this may be achieved with the help of books, films, any number of representations of the desired fulfilment, accompanied by masturbatory fancy. In my youth, this used to be called 'self-abuse' and one can see why it was regarded as sinful, for it, too, completely negates the spiritual element of existence and substitutes mere orgasmic release as the purpose. But at least it harms nobody but the solitary perpetrator. Real danger looms when the wish to have an unresisting partner is satisfied not by imagination, but by robbing the partner of the power to resist.

The sadist will seek to realise this state of affairs literally, by tying the partner down so that resistance is futile. In this way he is master of the event whatever happens. The partner (victim) may protest, cry, bewail, threaten, implore, all to no avail, for the sadist alone controls what will happen, when, and how. Indeed, the protestations fuel his desire, for they confirm his power, and the uselessness of refusal. The sadist contrives to turn the disaster of a refusal to his advantage, by making it part of the fulfilment he needs. Since he cannot enjoy the intense pleasure of reciprocity, he will make selfishness just as intense, and the partner's desire (or lack of it – that was the beginning of the sadistic journey) becomes irrelevant. In a peculiar way, the sadist is still part of a shared encounter, though skewed, because two people are involved; one of them, however, only as non-consenting recipient of the acts of the other.

It is one step further to silence all protest by making the partner dead. The necrophile is so terrified of having his advances rejected that he must make all rejection impossible. It is a pathetic, as well as a disgusting, derangement, for the necrophile will frequently take the arms of a corpse to embrace him in mock semblance of mutual love. This is the ultimate refuge of the inadequate and the fearful, and the ultimate manifestation of grotesque self-regard. No hatred, nor even dislike, of the murdered person is a necessary prelude to his death. Only the need to keep him quiet prevails. (In fact, Jeffrey Dahmer in Milwaukee only murdered men he liked, and his earlier crude attempts to copy love-making were with a mannequin from a shop-window and men so drugged and drunk they were comatose and therefore seeming-dead.)

Thus it can be seen that the abuse of pre-pubescent children may fit into this psychiatric pattern. There is no need to be sadistic, for children will be so scared and mystified by what is happening that they will not seek to escape, assuming, as they so often do, that the adult must know best and that his will anyway cannot be thwarted. So they are compliant through fear, which fuels the adult's perverted quest for spiritless, mechanical contact. The child becomes a mere object of lust, pornographic in the fullest sense because the living creature is reduced to an aid towards masturbation. There are some abusers who manage to mix this cruel exploitation with an added confection of fantasy, deluding themselves into thinking that the child enjoys being treated in this way. A man interviewed on television, after having served a prison term for child sex-abuse, still maintained that what he had experienced with an eight-year-old girl was not an enforcement of his will but a 'relationship', which she valued as much as he, and that the world had been woefully wrong to misinterpret it.

There is yet another possibility, less morally repugnant perhaps, but just as lamentable and worrying. Interfering with children could derive from a severely distorted version of a healthy human instinct, and one that is largely responsible for our huge success as a species – the need to experiment. Curiosity may be said to be the curse of human intelligence, as well as the motor of its progress. We can never rest until we find out more about how things work, how to invent other things which work better, and even how to manipulate other human beings. We start at this latter within minutes of birth, and spend most of our infancy learning what we can get away with and where to set the limits to our urge for self-expression. The emergence from this chaotic self-indulgence into responsible awareness of others is the beginning of maturity and morality. There are those, however, who never quite proceed this far, and remain long into adulthood with a child-like need to have their way and to claim personal freedom for any experiment they care to make which involves the freedom of others. This nasty aberration is carefully concealed (being in the head, being an inclination to certain activity, there is no reason why it should be visible or detectable without evidence), and the person so afflicted may have demanding and responsible employment, be a decent husband and father, and an otherwise helpful member of his community. He may even be publicly applauded for his achievements. But privately, like a child, he wants to see 'what would happen if', and his mania for experiment may extend to having sexual relations with children. Further, because he is stuck in this infantile mode, he will not emerge from it when curiosity is satisfied, but will endlessly repeat the behaviour, with a compulsiveness which is truly childish and staggeringly unresponsive to threat, reproof or punishment. The number of child molesters who have been revealed to be professional and intelligent men, or famous personalities, is itself surprising at first. But the greater shock is to discover how all-consuming the activity has been over many years, as is sometimes testified by enough pornographic material to fill a library. Any judge who tells such people that their interest in children is depraved and must be controlled is talking to the wall. Or rather to another child. They must do what they want to do, and that is that.

I have thought about these difficult and unpleasant subjects because they have often impinged upon the work I was doing, and I needed to know what I was talking about. Loud condemnation is not sufficient for a writer who wants to learn. Frederick West was a torturer and murderer who also looked upon his predatory conquest of his own daughters, from the age of eight onwards, as normal. Nobody could possibly have convinced him otherwise. In the years which separated Jeffrey Dahmer's first murder from his second, he was arrested for exposing himself in a public park, specifically to children; the one offence appeared to derive from the same disorder as the other. And, on the ground that an author's best subject is himself, I have occasionally been bound to look into my own character in a disquieting attempt to seek out any echoes.

At the trial of the Moors Murderers Ian Brady and Myra Hindley in 1966 there was one moment which has become fixed in folk memory as uniquely horrible. One of their victims was a little girl called Lesley Ann Downey.

Before Brady killed her, he had her undress and pose before his camera, while he taped her pathetic pleas to be allowed to go home to her mother. The tape was played in court, and everybody present was forced to imagine what suffering, what anguish of fear, the little girl endured. Nine photographs were taken of her, not especially monstrous, and she was not, as that 'folk memory' subsequently invented by vicious embellishment, tortured in any way. But she was hideously humiliated by an adult.

I was not myself abused as a child, and in view of the allegedly widespread practice of this abomination, I must count myself very fortunate. It was this freedom from taint which allowed me, I suppose, to view any attempt by a stranger to inveigle me into some naughty deed with wry amusement. The first memory I have of anything like it was in Brockwell Park, Herne Hill, in South London. It must have been when we were living nearby in Milkwood Road, which would place me at the age of seven. I was with another boy my own age, passing the time in the park, when a grown-up approached us and asked where the public toilets might be. I pointed out the direction to him, but this was not enough. He wanted me to show him where they were. So I led the way, my friend trailing behind. I must indeed have been naïve, for I have a secure recollection of my mood, which was one of wishing to help. The man seemed obviously old to me, but he might have been any age from twenty to fifty; one does not discern much at the age of seven. When we reached the toilets, he asked me to go in with him. At this point I suddenly felt there was more involved than giving information. I was apprehensive, but not fearful. My friend, rather more cautious, remained outside. The man went to the *pissoir* wall and made a half-move sideways to expose himself to me. That was too much. I averted my eyes before he could flash, so I cannot even say whether the sight shook me; I saw nothing. I also shifted myself closer to the door, thinking there might be reason for escape at any minute. But still I was not afraid. I just thought this behaviour a bit odd (like almost everyone in those days, I had never seen either of my parents naked). Then he asked if I did want to see anything. I said I wanted to see his bum. Whereupon he lowered his trousers and presented me with a vision of flesh, and I fled immediately, grabbing my friend's arm and running until we were out of the park on the pavement, happily surrounded by other people. Still, I did not feel fear. I laughed.

What I did feel was that what had happened would have to be kept secret. Neither of us must ever tell our parents. This reaction is interesting for several reasons. It first shows that not all flashers are harmful. It would have been a different matter if I had been made to perform a sexual act myself, but as it was even I could see that the incident was ridiculous. It also shows why so many child-molesters are not apprehended, for they are protected by the children themselves, not always out of fear, but because the children would not know how to set about telling grown-ups what has occurred. They do not have the vocabulary for it, and do not want to have their ignorance exposed by anticipated questioning. Better to keep quiet. And it lastly shows, or rather at least suggests, that if the vast array of child pornography now zipping down telephone wires to home computers everywhere were available to that poor man in 1946, his ambitions might not have stopped at flashing. I talked earlier of the purity of the child. Remembering Brockwell Park, and the feelings the incident induced, I am quite sure that the man intended no assault upon my purity. He was perhaps of the last category I considered, the grown-up with infantile curiosity. Had I encouraged him, would he have edged further into experiment? Who knows! But I do not think his intentions were malign. And my response was not perverse.

Three years later a different kind of attempted seduction left me rather more concerned. I was an inveterate cinema-goer, and often caught up with films which were not sufficiently popular to be shown to great audiences, but could be found in smaller cinemas off the beaten track. One such was at Camberwell Green, at the beginning of Camberwell Road opposite the bus terminal (which is still there). Here I went one afternoon and found myself a seat in a row near the front, with nobody else in sight. There were perhaps half a dozen other people in the cinema, all many rows behind me at the back. It was as if I had the film all to myself.

Until a man came and sat beside me. Once again, ludicrous ignorance protected me from any worry. I was mystified why he should have chosen that particular seat when there were hundreds more he could have taken and been more private, but that was his business, and I wanted to watch the film. I was not concerned about him. And yet. I know that I noticed enough, this time, to assess his age by the shape and size of the shadowy figure next to me, and he was in his twenties. And when his seat began to shake I knew that he was there not by accident, but precisely to be near to me. His hand appeared in the gloom before and below me, and I could see he was rubbing two coins together. I pushed them away, with coy indignation, and actually spoke to him, saying that I wanted to watch the film and would he please leave me alone. But he could not be deterred. I glanced down to my left. He had opened his fly-buttons and was masturbating himself, protected from view on the other side by his coat held in place for the purpose. By now it was more difficult to concentrate on the film, but I maintained my fixed purpose to do so, and would not be tempted by his bribery. The money would have been very useful, but nothing on earth would have allowed me to touch him, which is what he wanted. His member was bigger than I had ever thought possible, which alone merited a second glance (seeing is believing), but I had emerged from infancy into childhood by this time, and dimly perceived that some-thing dreadful was about to happen. Besides, I simply did not *want* to touch. I moved to another seat some rows behind, not before giving him a piece of my mind, to the effect that he was spoiling my afternoon (!), and continued to watch the film. He, too chastened to pursue me in an empty cinema, I suppose, left. But this time I could not laugh. My mind was full of it. For the first time I was aware that I, a mere boy, could be alluring, though why or how I could not conceive. A door had opened.

This story has a point, too. I was not abused by the stranger, but he had invaded my imagination with his unhappy soul, given me more to think about than was good for me. So, in that way, he had assailed my purity, and I came out of that encounter less pure than I had been before. I was a subtly different person, and he had been the agent of that change. By what right? None at all. What the story teaches me is that all those thousands of children below the age of twelve who are depicted in pornographic poses can in no measure at all be willing parties to what is occurring to them. They simply do not know what it is all about, and are obeying orders incom-prehensible to them. I am told by policemen who have seen these pictures that the fear in the eyes of the children is palpable and haunting. I can well understand it should be so. Had the man in the cinema taken me somewhere by force and made me commit acts which meant nothing to me, beyond a certain forbidden prurience, I should have been terrified. It may even be a premature fear of death, for if adults were capable of these impossibly dirty acts, they could be capable of anything. And had the man in Brockwell Park kidnapped me and made me see him, I should have died of shame. What these men do is slip in a poisonous pin of wonder where total ignorance obtained, and thereby press adult concerns upon people far too young to know how to cope with them. I do distinctly recall telling myself, in the deep quietness of private thought, that whatever happened I would never permit myself to become a 'dirty old man'.

By the time of the next surreptitious encounter, also in a cinema, I was already pubescent, when keen eagerness to find out more had wiped out all timid prevarication. There were two very popular cinemas at the Elephant and Castle opposite one another, and they appeared to be full every night. At times I found all seats sold and had disconsolately to take the bus back to Albany Road. This time I was there for a Doris Day film, always a sell-out, and I got in. The man seated next to me indicated an interest, but I was able to deflect him by frank admission that I would prefer to see the film, thank you very much, if only he would wait. He extracted from me a promise to go home with him afterwards, then he kept quiet. We took the bus from outside the cinema down to the Old Kent Road, where we were evidently seen by somebody, because my mother confronted me with this the following day, and I told her he wanted to show me his stamp-collection. It sounds risible now, and I imagine it must have done so then, but she did not know how, or whether, to push her enquiries, so the matter was dropped. There is even the possibility that she was wise enough to realise that no harm had been done and that a boy must grow up somehow, but I rather doubt it; the question of homosexual behaviour was entirely foreign to her understanding. The stranger, again in his twenties, did not impose. On the contrary, he was happy to restrict the level of involvement to whatever I found unthreatening, which meant that I merely gawped and gazed for a while, feeding my eyes with an unaccustomed vision. I certainly did not touch him, although he may well have fondled me. It was a small squalid room which served as kitchen and sitting-room, quite common in the cramped conditions of post-war London, and he asked me to keep quiet as his mother was asleep in the room immediately behind the door. I soon left and walked home to Herring Street. The important ingredient of this event is its plaintive innocence. I imagine it might be called child-abuse by some, although there was not a moment when I felt in danger or under coercion. At fourteen I was inquisitive and ready for some experience, however petty and foolish, so my consent was not in doubt. I was party to the molestation which occurred.

In those days there was never overt mention in newspapers of any sexual offence before the courts, whether from concern for the sensibilities of the reader or by order of the judge I know not, which meant that everything had to be said in code and mountains of interpretation could be piled upon the use of a single word. The *News of the World*, always the most prurient newspaper in Britain, as well as the best-selling, reported every week cases of defendants accused of 'interfering with' a boy or girl, and one had to wonder exactly what that might involve. Well, if it involved the sort of fumbling which I witnessed in a grubby kitchen off the Old Kent Road, then it did not amount to much. All this is worth recounting for the conclusion to which it must draw us. I have an overwhelming feeling that the degree of sexual assault upon young people then, and the degree which obtains now with those revolting scenes on computer screens, are as far removed one from the other as are the modest coverings placed over piano legs in Victorian times from the quasi-nudity which teenage girls display as a matter of course today. We have, in other words, passed through a revolution in sexual crime. The widespread exploitation of children which we hear of now is almost a new phenomenon, or at least the epidemic proportions it has gathered are new. I am aware that I am arguing from too few instances, and a statistical researcher would not be impressed by a case which presents so little evidence, but I suspect such research would bear me out. The world of today is severely diseased in this regard. The world through which I passed was, by comparison, rather hesitant and subdued.

It was even easy enough to see off a predator by oneself. One particular individual, who started a conversation with me at the bus-stop on Camberwell Green as I waited for the No 42 to take me home after school, became a bit of a pest. He was tall and robust, with huge thick spectacles like the bottom of a bottle, an insidious, ingratiating manner, and a delicacy of speech which belied his gross and greasy appearance. He was also of a persistence fit to earn medals. Having contrived to sit next to me on the bus, he then made sure he was at the same bus-stop every day, until I told him to keep away. He took to lurking near the school-gates so he could catch me on the way down Camberwell Church Street towards the Green and indulge in desultory conversation, as if we were chums who frequently chatted like this. I was embarrassed lest I be observed by my contemporaries being pursued by this ogre, and persuaded him to desist. He graduated into becoming my entry-ticket to films which were certified for children only when accompanied by an adult (harmless things, really, perhaps containing some grim battle-scenes), and would often be at the cinema waiting to see if I would turn up, so that he could take my money and buy the ticket for me. More pretended conversation would ensue, until I told him, with cruel ardour, to piss off.

It would never have occurred to me to report him to the police. Nor did I ever feel the need for 'counselling', which did not then exist in its ubiquitous modern form, where even a splinter from a wood-shaving requires advice from a 'counsellor' as to how to deal with the trauma. Then, you had parents, teachers, the family doctor, all of whom would have been useless in dealing with the problem of a pathetic predator. I had to deal with it myself, and in so doing, learnt a little bit more about survival. Years later, as an adult, I encountered this man again quite by chance and went to Lyon's Corner House with him for a cup of tea. He seemed even more hopeless, a shuffling apology of a man, and I felt some kind of pity for him. I began to realise that this was the sort of obsessive who was fingered by the *News of the World* in their reports of 'interference', the text-book copy of the paederast who feverishly sought the friend-ship of adolescent boys. And this frightened me, at last, because I discerned that this was the sort of man I could become.

As the routine romantic friendships of schooldays took their course, I did not care to look to the future to see what might replace them. I doubt whether boys do make plans much beyond tea-time, anyway. But I realised there was something noticeably more intense and enduring about my attachments, while to my contemporaries they amounted to little more than larking about or exploring the games of affection, the heady pleasures of 'touching', and the black moods of possession which followed in their wake. My friends all seemed to pass easily from mild sexual romps at school to more of the same with the local girlfriend at home. I did not. My romps were not so mild, and there was no girlfriend in Herring Street waiting to redress the balance.

Anxious to see where I was going, I read as many books as I could on the subject, mostly in the admirable Penguin series published under the Pelican imprint. There were titles on adolescent sexuality, on Ancient Greek customs, and one seminal work by Margaret Mead (since, I believe, somewhat discredited), called *Coming of Age in Samoa*, which promised that if one went to the Pacific Islands one would find encouragement rather than prohibition. The upshot of all this study was the expectation that I would 'grow out of' this temporary phase like everybody else. The trouble was, I showed no signs of so doing. I went secretly to see the local doctor, and told him of my apprehensions, which were, without doubt, quite severe. Though I cannot recall what I said, I have the distinct feel in my memory of the worry and confusion which occupied my thoughts every day, and of the fear that I would somehow end up *abnormal*. The doctor told me to go away and play more football, which was a fat lot of use.

Confirmation of my suspicions came during my year in Montpellier and the beginning of that searing attachment to Jean-Philippe which I have recounted in another book.

In summary, I spent ten months of my university degree course teaching English conversation and grammar at two boys' schools in Montpellier. At one of them, I became friendly with the headmaster's secretary, who had three sons, aged eleven, thirteen and fourteen. Her husband, a soldier, had been killed the year before in France's colonial war with Algeria; she did not know how or why. So when I went to Algeria during the Easter break, I insinuated myself with the military and tracked down the man who had been with Monsieur in his jeep when the bomb exploded beneath them, and thus I was able to give Madame the details which the authorities had kept from her, through indifference more than neglect. Ever after, I dined at their house at least once a week, treated the boys as my younger brothers, while their mother treated me as an extra son. To this day, more than forty years later, I still call her 'Maman'.

Jean-Philippe was the middle one of the three. When I finally left Montpellier, the whole family came to the railway-station to send me off. I saw that Jean-Philippe, uncharacteristically, was in floods of tears.

Three years later, I returned for a visit. There was no spare bedroom, so 'Maman' said I would have to share a bed with Jean-Philippe. It was then, after three or four nights, that he began silently to demonstrate his affection. I shall never forget the one sentence he uttered in the dark: 'Why did you wait three years before coming back?' Thereafter, I visited frequently.

The fact that the friendship was initiated by him, then promoted by him, and finally consummated by him, is how it should be, for I was by then over twenty and would have been at fault (though not apparently in Samoa or Periclean Athens) had I been the active seducer of a sixteen-year-old. At least I had escaped the scourge of predation. But it was by now absolutely obvious that there was no 'growing out of' this preference for male romance. I was stuck, and I would have to adapt as best I could.

Four years later Jean-Philippe married, and I went over to France to be Best Man at the wedding. The feast was inter-minable – eleven courses over a period of some four hours – and I left the table to stretch my legs and relieve what was frankly an attack of boredom. So did Jean-Philippe's new brother-in-law, a lively, mercurial, mischievous lad called François, then aged about thirteen. We took the dogs for a stroll and chatted ceaselessly, both happy to be free of the formality of a sit-down meal which promised never to end. On my return to England, we began a correspondence, and over the following four years he became a visitor, coming to stay with me two or three times a year for a week or two. He said he wanted to 'try everything', and so I was to be the means of this determined education. Again, he was the instigator, but there was a sense in which I had crossed the line between accidental connection and active pursuer, for it was I who had seduced him with attention, with letters and invitations, to the point where his final eruption into sexual play of his own volition was almost inevitable; it no longer required any suggestion from me. I believe this is what professionals whose job it is to spot and stop so-called paedophiles term 'grooming'. I see what they mean. I had slowly prepared François to select himself as my lover.

Nevertheless, I felt, and still feel, no guilt in the affair. At no point was François coerced or threatened. Nor even was he persuaded by tactile conquest. He simply blossomed into the person he wanted to be, knowing that I would not reject or ridicule him. The extent of my 'grooming' must be that I planted that knowledge within him, giving him the courage to be himself in full confidence of my friendship.

It was a volatile relationship, for François was highly-strung, nerveux, prone to anger and sulks and volcanic displays of displeasure (it was to be my fate, probably self-inflicted, always to drift towards such people), and even though his visits were over in a matter of days, they left in their wake whole ship-wrecks of emotional débris. Still, I was able to offer him a side of sophisticated London life that would not otherwise have come his way. This was the period of my close friendship with the ballerina Doreen Wells, and François became an admirer of hers, watching her dance frequently at Covent Garden. He was also enchanted with the restaurant San Lorenzo in Beauchamp Place, and when, some thirty years later, I took him there again with his wife and son, Mara, the owner and glorious hostess, grabbed him in a warm, sloppy Italian embrace. I have never seen anyone look so happy; François beamed with delight. He also met the girl I should have married, Camilla, and he always hoped that I would ask her to be my wife.

He married twice, and his son is now a grown man. I still see him from time to time, where he runs a sea-food restaurant on the Mediterranean coast and has his own oyster-farm. Apparently he told his brother-in-law Jean-Philippe, years ago, that he had had a relationship with me, and Jean-Philippe was able to reveal that he had beaten him to it. A silly story, perhaps, but I tell it only to give the reader a flavour of the harmlessness of these events. I can never recognise myself in the horror stories that I read of mature men corrupting and despoiling youth, forcing sex upon boys who should be at the beginning of adventure, not thrown so early into the pit of degradation. It is sickening to me that such men are nowadays always referred to as *paedophiles*, when they can be nothing of the sort, for they do not love youth, but besmirch it for their selfish gratification.

Paedophilia used to be a respectable word with a scientific pedigree and a proper meaning. Its etymological roots are Greek and Latin, and they may offer the rough translation 'love of youth'. But this, as Oscar Wilde discovered to his final cost, is imprecise at best, and at worst falls hostage to wilful misinterpretation. Illiterate journalists now take for granted what they think is meant here by 'love', and legislators, who used to be well-educated, have blindly followed suit. In fact, any decent schoolmaster or youth-club steward, or even father, must be a paedophile or he is nothing. If you take your job of educating the young, guiding their amusements or bringing them up at home as merely tasks devoid of deep personal involvement, you will not achieve much. Indeed, you may do much harm. It is essential that these endeavours be pursued with love and attention, that their outcome matters on an emotional as well as professional level, that the commitment of the father, the teacher, the scoutmaster, be grounded in affectionate concern for the well-being and emerging maturity of their charges. They should really *love* to see boys develop and get better at whatever they are doing or thinking, challenge their minds and imaginations, stretch their physical capacities, spread wide their search for experience. To watch a person grow in the knowledge that you have helped in his development from amorphous tyro into self-confident mini-adult is very gratifying. And if this pleasure contains an element of affection, so be it. Were the affection lacking, the development might well be arid and mechanical. There are many people, myself included, who can remember a particular teacher having a particular influence which changed the course of their mental life; it does not take a step of much courage to grant that the attention thus received was a version of loving kindness, of selflessness devoted to the education, the growing-up, of another being. That should be the description of a paedophile.

Instead, we get the cheap and crude impression of dirty old men in raincoats or, worse, people engaged in criminal sexual assault. These are the type of people the Sunday papers glory in hunting down, for the shabby delectation of their readers and the delight of their bankers. But they are not paedophiles. They are perverts. They have no love for youth; what they have is an obsession with sexual domination, which is fed by using the youth in question as a prop, an object, a fetish. When, in late adolescence, I anguished over whether I should become a dirty old man, and how I could stop the process, I did not understand these distinctions, or I need not have worried. I should already have known that I was inclined towards genuine paedophilia, for I was undoubtedly interested in the young. And only a few years later my experience would have confirmed that the inclination endured, with splendid and triumphant results. But I should also have known that I could never be party to the corruption of youth. The one is nourishment, the other poison.

It would be otiose to bring in support of this view the dozens of writers and poets who have given far better expression to it than I can, but the subject has been celebrated for centuries. Some of Shakespeare's very sonnets are paedophilic in tone, openly desiring the young friend's emergence into manhood and happiness, and feeling at ease with a parallel expression of admiration for him. The fusion of love and education are explicit in the hope that the young man will marry and sew his goodness in fatherhood – you cannot be much more paedo-philic than that. The so-called Uranian poets at the end of the nineteenth century paraded boy-love rather more remotely, as they would need to in an age devoted to the refinement of hypocrisy. And a little-known poet of the twentieth century, Ralph Chubb, perfectly distils the essential decency of this kind of admiration and, at the same time, its undercurrent of immaturity. His poems, now collector's items, were for the most part privately published, and illustrated with his own spare, idealistic, affectionate yet quietly erotic pencil drawings of boys' heads, as far removed from pornography as is a Barbara Cartland novel.

Of course, the best expression of the ideal is in Ancient Greek literature, in the conversations of Plato and Socrates or the writings of the great dramatists. Anyone who reads these with independent mind will immediately spot the ingredient in this love which is its most salient characteristic, namely the spiritual. One invites ridicule these days by use of such a word in such a context, but it is evident the Greeks did not think it at all a laughing matter. Their friendships for adolescent young men were noble and responsible, born of a devotion to the ideal of spiritual, emotional and intellectual education. Their friend-ships with their womenfolk were procreational, with their men-friends recreational. We are right to have jettisoned the Greek attitude towards wives and slaves as insulting to the spirit of mankind. But to chuck away the paedophilic element as well seems to me an impoverishment.

To return to my clumsy bus-stop pursuer a few pages back, in the light of these reflections I can now see that he was predatory by default. What he really wanted was an opportunity for innocent attachment, to be a sort of *précepteur* towards me, to click on to that elusive, spiritual, invisible, mostly unattainable connection between people responsibly involved. It eluded him not only because I mocked and derided him (not then understanding as I do now), but also because he had not the subtlety to appreciate his own deep-seated motives. But I was wrong to mock. He was not a child-abuser. Those wretched people do not assert the spiritual, they destroy it. There could be no greater chasm between the two, and it is thoughtless, even wicked, to confuse them.

I suppose much of the foregoing informed my fostering of Gary, my one (I hope worthy) attempt at surrogate fatherhood. I have written about him several times already, and devoted one book entirely to the story of his place in my life, so I must not repeat. A few comments only are called for in the light of what I have tried to say thus far.

He was, simply, the most needy person I had ever encountered. He came to me because his step-grandfather, a London guide, was destined to look after him one day and had therefore to abandon the job he was due to take on for my bunch of tourists. The boy never went to school, so somebody had to stay with him, I was told. I said that I could not replace him as guide, so why not let me look after his grandson for the day? Thus does Fate creep in, unannounced.

There followed three years of scorching difficulty, as I struggled to give Gary a framework to his life, to learn the business of fatherhood from scratch, to claim his allegiance and devote attention to him, to watch him stumble painfully from a world of zero achievement towards a world in which he might hold some pride. In return for his taking over the guest-room in my house, I insisted he went to school, and spent many an hour discussing his problems with teachers. He was inordinately brave, because what he wanted most was to be able to show me how well he was doing, and yet, being almost illiterate, he was bound to be at the bottom of the class. His frustrations and disappointments must have been gigantic, and he naturally vented them against the world, with mendacity, violent tantrums, dangerous explosions of pent-up wrath. It was an arduous journey which we took together, my-self through choice, he through need. Looking back, of course I should never have done it; it was presumptuous, to say the least, to imagine that I could. But at the time, it was urgent. Gary simply could not, must not, be plunged into yet another disappointment. I could not turn my back upon him.

Had Gary been sexually adventurous, as François was, there would have been a catastrophic personal tragedy for him as a direct consequence of the fostering experiment, because he needed something far more precious and more profound, which a friendship would have destroyed. He was fourteen, a virtual orphan with bitter, crippling memories. His parents had married young, when neither was responsible or committed to a future. They separated amid furious rancour and the man disappeared. Gary never knew him. He and his mother had moved back to her parents, that is her mother and stepfather. Thus the young mother was once more treated with the in-dulgence of a child, while she had a child herself. She was irredeemably dissolute and sexually greedy, so that her infant son grew up witnessing her being abused by an endless sequence of strange men, for she enjoyed physical maltreat-ment. She was also often drunk, with no time for Gary at all. Within a couple of years she was dead, the consequence, I believe, of a fall down a whole flight of stairs. She was only in her twenties, and Gary may well have seen what happened. I know that he was forever haunted by memories of his mother, and would not hear a word said against her without the pupils of his eyes dilating and a dangerous anger mounting.

The grandmother was the most disastrously kind woman I have ever met. I watched as she allowed Gary to move unwanted food from his plate on to hers, as she handed him money to squander every day, as she acquiesced in his chronic truancy the better to please him. He was therefore almost totally illiterate and completely dependent upon her for emotional sustenance, which meant subservience. He had never formed an attachment to anyone else. He had never been disciplined, by which I mean that nobody had ever suggested to him that it mattered to somebody what he said and what he did, that he could produce happiness or pain by his behaviour. He had never even been told what time to come home at night. Nothing had any weight in his life. He floated in a void of gratification. He was, in the quiet corner of his soul, miserable and abandoned.

Gary desperately needed somebody to tell him what to do, to earn praise when it was merited and chastisement when it was needed. He wanted, in short, a father, and as soon as he realised that I was loose (which I swear he did within hours of our first encounter – the emptiness of his emotional life had made him astonishingly acute and alert), he grabbed the chance of a pretend one. That same day he commandeered a room in my house for himself, wrote his name on the door of it, and left in it some of his belongings. Also on the first day he sought permissions, testing when he might be allowed to smoke, when he should go out, and whether I would help him go to school by going to see the headmaster on his behalf. His needs were so blatant, so urgent, and writ so large, that it was impossible to refuse them without damage.

The rest, as I say, is a long story, but let us consider what might have occurred had he used sexual allure as one bait to get what he so frantically required. The confusion in his mind between fatherhood and friendship would have had a potential to derail him into yet worse avenues, to have muddled his affections and taught him the power of enticement and seduction in human affairs. He might have become a grotesque exploiter of adult weaknesses. I am eternally grateful that none of this was ever a danger, for I cannot be certain that I should have been able to deflect him as I ought. Our relationship was patent and clear, and when the authorities proposed that I legitimise it by officially fostering him, Gary was overjoyed. I had misgivings, because he was a handful and I was inexperienced, untrained for these eventualities, but I knew I must accept the responsibilities, for I had made implicit promises by inviting his trust in the first place.

And here is the crucial point I wish to make. It is possible for a paedophilic interest to be channelled away from fondness and tactile encounter into a sublimated form of affection which is ultimately both more valuable and more durable. Had I not been susceptible to adolescent male charm I might not have noticed him in the first place; but because I was so susceptible I was ready to do everything I could to help him grow into a healthy undamaged adult. It certainly was a case of a man in his thirties taking to live with him a boy in his teens, but so far removed from child-abuse that child-enhancement would have been a better description. Attraction may have been the point of departure, but it was quickly diverted and converted into parental delight.

Of course, I may even now, more than thirty years later, be deluding myself to some extent. I can never know how much Gary intuited my nature, for we never discussed such matters, myself purposefully avoiding them and he apparently uninterested in them. But perhaps he knew more than he divulged. If so, then he was self-taught in maturity, for his manifest concerns were more infantile, making up for the childhood he had missed. He wanted to be tucked up in bed, to be made comfy and clean. If he was able to receive all these attentions from me, while still knowing in his heart that I was capable of others which I kept out of the frame, then he was wise indeed. There are mysterious depths in every human personality.

Gary eventually left the 'pretend' home when he moved in with his girlfriend in the East End, as yet another surrogate son to her parents (telling me that it was a chance to have both a mum and a dad, and he was getting on, so the opportunity would not occur again). He was, then, not asexual, and he went on to become a father twice before he was twenty. Quite apart from all the other lessons which this long and troubled period of my life brought home to me, the one that pertains most to this chapter is the potentially beneficent application of a paedophilic nature.

On the other hand, I would be obtuse to a degree if I did not acknowledge that some vicious and disgusting crimes are committed by men mistakenly (in my view) labelled paedophiles. The gang of brutes who sodomised and suffocated Jason Swift, a hungry and willing fourteen-year-old in Hackney in 1989 were murderers intoxicated with sexual power, who had no regard for the boy as a person with wishes and restraints and fears of his own; after sex, they strangled him, and served far too short a term in prison for their pitiless barbarity. There is nobody who would spare a word in their defence, even were it important to study their mentality for the purposes of deepening our knowledge of the aberrations of mankind, a fact amply supported by the open contempt shown towards such men by other prisoners, themselves often serving time for murder.

I have never been called upon to write about such a case as the murder of Jason Swift, but a number of other cases have brought some manifestation of child-abuse to my notice, and I have struggled to make sense of them. Frederick West turned his own eight-year-old daughter into his clandestine mistress, regularly subjecting her to full sexual lust until he finally impregnated her at the age of sixteen. The little girl, of course, had no means of knowing that what her father demanded of her was unusual; she assumed that was what Daddy did, and since she wanted above all to please him, she smothered her inchoate feeling that it was wrong. She was his only daughter by his first marriage, and she resented her stepmother Rosemary's intervention between them. Obliging her father was one sure way to cement her special relationship with him. He was a moral regenerate from the backwoods, who thought it proper he should be the first to teach sexual pleasure to his daughters, because boys would not know how to go about it. Thus the girl grew into puberty and adolescence with a turmoil of confused and conflicting emotions from which she has never since recovered. He murdered her soul.

And what of the scores of murders committed by John Wayne Gacy in a Chicago suburb in the 1970s? All were adolescent boys. All were killed by this man in fulfilment of some dreadful pornographic fantasy, or in pursuit of some addiction to power, their bodies then stuffed into the cellar, under the floor or in the garden. His was in no way a paedophilic nature – it was a destructive nature; the two words are mutually exclusive. Gacy's passion was satanic.

That purity of which I spoke at the beginning of this chapter was never so perfectly portrayed as in the two sweet little girls Holly and Jessica, cruelly slaughtered by Ian Huntley in Soham, Cambridgeshire. I know but little of their characters, only what I read in the newspapers in fact, but I was present at the reconstruction of their disappearance, snatched from the road into thin air, which the police arranged in order to enlist public help. Two other ten-year-olds were dressed exactly as Holly and Jessica had been, with identical football T-shirts, taking the ordinary route through their home town towards an extraordinary and unimaginable fate. We saw them turn a corner into our view and walk briskly, nonchalantly down the road towards us. They were happy and carefree. They were not lost, they had done no wrong, they were not yet missing from home; they were just out for a walk and a chatter. The burden of knowing a destiny of which they were blissfully ignorant fell upon us, the witnesses, the Greek chorus, and I was choked and tearful in the contemplation of this cruel absurdity. They would never be seen again, by anyone, save of course the man who despatched them out of life. There before us, in this recon-struction, was the vision of purity about to be defiled. At no other time have I felt so keenly the wickedness of an adult pressing his needs upon the unsuspecting, uncomprehending simplicity of a child. It is the triumph of guile over artlessness, and one which is utterly shameful.

No wonder I have at times looked in upon myself and imagined that others might well see the very nastiness which I deplore. After all, I am a man who has had affectionate relation-ships of differing descriptions with three young men; need one look any further? Yes, one does so need. In fact, one must. The division between those who follow a conventional path and those others who deviate into less certain territory is a subtle one, to do with character, ambition, the will to face surprises. That other division, between people, on the one hand, who are incapable of escaping from self, who cannot look outwards, who can sacrifice all moral nuance and all consideration for others upon the altar of their malignant needs; and on the other hand those who subordinate immediate satisfactions to the more patient urge to do good, to encourage and foster, that is the division which matters. To have led a life which is in some measure different from the norm requires constant self-awareness and attention, self-questioning and investigation, and very little self-regard. To stay on that road with clear sight requires the gift of that abstract comfort which Catholics call grace.

My relationships with women have all been touched with an ease of flirtation, coupled with a paradoxical reluctance to see the flirtation through to a conclusion, and one in particular was suffused with that grace which made of every meeting a sweet pleasure and renewal of attachment. In fact, it still is. I refer, of course, to Camilla. But that belongs to another book.

CHAPTER SIX

More People

I remember the date and the place. It was 16 July 1966, and we were dining at a restaurant, long since gone, called Inigo Jones, at the bottom corner of Floral Street immediately opposite the Garrick Club. I was taken to dinner by Jim Branciforti and Bob Covais, who were both at the peak of a successful cycle in the travel business in America and were over in London for a brief break. They had experienced the troughs before, and would sink into them again later, but they held to the sane view that while you have money you should enjoy it. So they spent far too much on a posh dinner, considering we were all still in our twenties and ought perhaps to have been frugal.

The big shock was the wine. Inigo Jones had a huge list, and Bob devoured every page, until he alighted upon a name which made him shriek with the passion of surprise discovery. He had found a bottle of Romanée-Conti. The year may have been 1949, but frankly that was a detail lost on me when I was too young to register such things. Indeed, I had nursed a silly prejudice against people who rhapsodised about wines and their nose and their bouquet and their rosemary-echoed velvet hues, all of which language I dismissed as deeply pretentious, the sort of rubbish Waugh might put into the mouth of a Sebastian Flyte but which had no place in the vocabulary of sensible souls. Wine was for drinking, I opined, not for chattering about.

Well, this was the day that caused an earthquake in my attitude towards wine. Each sip was such a sumptuous delight, such ecstatic stroking of the taste-buds, such a rush up the back of my head, that I saw at once why good wine kills conversation, for there is absolutely nothing else to talk about. To have a mouthful and not pay tribute to it, be it merely in the thwarted attempt to describe it, would have been insulting, unthinkable. So all three of us talked about the wine we were drinking, and not a word passed our lips about life and loves. I have since found out, of course, that Romanée-Conti is so rarely found on a list because it is produced in such small quantities, all coming from one tiny field (which I have now seen) near Vosne-Romanée north of Beaune. It was twenty-five years before I spotted the name again, and that was in a Berry Bros and Rudd catalogue. I was so excited, I decided that I would order some as a treat for myself, and perhaps even drink it alone, despite the fact that it was listed at £500, which was ten times what I would normally pay for a case. I telephoned to reserve. The Berry Bros assistant, with enormous courtesy and tact, found a way to make clear to me that the cost was actually £500 a *bottle*. Of course, I did not buy it, and may never have a second bottle in my life. At the time of writing, the price has soared to thousands. However, when I know my time has come, I might throw away enough of the inheritance to spoil myself with one of those again, as well as a Château Petrus and a Château La Tache for good measure.

From abject ignorance I advanced to pretended sage, giving lectures on how to store, judge and taste wine to my annual students from Tennessee at a wine-tasting in Beaune. I know very little, but my appreciation and palpable pleasure in the subject carry the day.

It is astonishing how many of those who can afford good wine persist in providing inferior stuff, not only for their guests, but for themselves. In some cases it is because they genuinely cannot tell one wine from another; I had one acquaintance, discerning in most other regards (but not, I recall, in how to choose friends, which may well be significant), who only drank the cheapest Valpolicella since a good Château Palmer tasted exactly the same to him. He was not mean, but possessed of a strong practical streak. I suspect that in order to get excited about wine one must needs be a romantic. Others I have known who, while pretending to a glittering social table in the tradition of the great society hostesses of the past, nevertheless provided indifferent wine precisely because they did not want to spend money in climbing the ladder, but preferred to get there on the cheap. One such was Tony Mayer.

I first met Tony when I organised the French Club at University College, Cardiff, as a green and silly youth of nineteen. We had an annual dinner at the Park Hotel, and my job was to invite a Guest Speaker. A recently published book called *La Vie Anglaise*, translated from the French, having originally been published in the *Que Sais-Je?* series which was highly valued in France, had attracted much attention and lengthy reviews for its amused account of the absurdities and anomalies of English life and customs. It was in the tradition of George Mikes. The author, Tony Mayer, turned out to be the Cultural Attaché at the French Embassy and therefore, I suppose, saw it as an integral part of his job to accept my invitation. I booked him a room at the hotel and a seat on the train from London. He presented me with a taxi fare in London as well. That ought to have been a hefty clue.

The talk passed off well, and Tony asked me to keep in touch. If ever I were to find myself in London, he and his wife Thérèse would be delighted to have me to dinner. A couple of years later I was indeed living in London, and announced my presence, but no invitation arrived. Until, that is, I happened to mention my friends in the Royal Ballet, for what reason I know not, probably because we were all going to the same performance, and then the invitations piled in. The Mayers liked to give after-theatre suppers on the top floor of their house in Chester Square, and they worked on a reputation for having present the actors, dancers, musicians or whatever following their performance on stage or platform. Why the top floor, which was cramped like an attic, and where the dining-table and chairs barely fitted the room, presenting frequent peril to the servants squeezing by with laden plates? After all, those Grosvenor houses in Chester Square were all built on a vast scale, over five floors, and had been suited from their inception to the provision of lavish hospitality. The Mayers had discovered that by subletting most of the house to wealthy bankers and living as squatters at the top, they could add remarkably to their savings. Another clue.

One of the dancers they wanted to invite was Doreen Wells, whom I then knew better than most. Tony implored me to persuade her to come to supper. There would be twelve at table, and, naturally, I was invited, too. (Excluding me would have been a difficult one to pull off, but I bet he and his wife pondered the possibility.) It was a late supper, dancers always taking an hour or so to scrape off their slap and get back into normal skin, so we could not have arrived before 11.30 p.m. Everybody else was there, eagerly waiting. I was taken aside. 'Brian, something rather tricky has happened. I do hope you can help. One of the guests has turned up with somebody else. We could not very well turn them away, so we have found a chair for the extra. But that makes thirteen, which we cannot have together at a table, don't you see? Bad luck, and all that. So would you mind eating at a little table by yourself in the next room? The menu will be exactly the same.'

Fuck the menu, I thought, but I was too young even to have *esprit d'escalier*, so I protested neither then nor afterwards. But I have protested ever since, to myself, and remain transfixed with amazement, flabbergasted indeed, that anyone should feel able to behave in such a way. And all without the slightest flicker of embarrassment.

I went to Chester Square more than once thereafter, and was properly seated on subsequent occasions. Then came the day for Tony to take his retirement from the Embassy and return to live in France.

It was, of course, a major upheaval to pack up the bits and pieces of a long career and married life, in which I played no part. But there came the time when, the inhabitants already departed, their big house was left empty, quiet and drab, yet still with some bed-linen and curtains folded in cupboards which had been left behind in the scramble. Tony called to ask if I would do him the favour of returning to Chester Square to pack up what was left and have it posted to Ménerbes in Provence. The whole lot filled about a dozen boxes, and it would be no easy matter to get these to a post-office; I was still in my twenties, with no motor-car. I told him, therefore, that although I could spend a day packing and labelling everything, I would need to get a taxi for transportation, and he agreed that I could do so at his expense. The precise amount of the taxi-fare was subsequently sent to me by money-order, which I was obliged to take to the post-office to be cashed. It seemed there was no limit to the amount of displacement I could be asked to endure. Worse than that, inside the envelope with the money-order was a scrap of paper with Tony's handwriting upon it, *Bon pour une cravate.* This, he explained, was a voucher for me alone. I could take it to a named shop in the King's Road, Chelsea, and choose a tie from a selection to be offered up to a certain value.

At last I found my voice. I sent the scrap of paper back to him with a note from myself saying that, if he wished to make me a gift, he should take the trouble to go out and buy it himself.

I also told him that I had noticed a chandelier hanging mournfully in one of the deserted rooms at Chester Square which he evidently did not want. I gathered it was Czecho-slovakian and reasonably modern, 1930s probably. Since I could see no reason why the new tenants should grab this for themselves, and since I needed something to hang in my study at Caithness Road, I had taken it down and transferred it from his house to mine, in another taxi which I paid for myself, where it would be very happy. Tony told me that I could buy the chandelier from him for £20. I decided to treat the cold effrontery of this remark with the disdain of silence, and never mentioned the subject to him again.

I have said that Tony and Thérèse retired to their home in Ménerbes. This delightful little hill-town, an utter jewel of rustic elegance, has since become far too famous as the result of a best-selling (and awful) book by one Peter Mayle. Crowds now march through it like a lava-flow, and the people who have lived there, in families stretching back through centuries of generations, are heartily sick of them. In the 1960s it was still peaceful, remote, untouched by vulgarity, and exerting a charm so powerful it almost hurt. I know because I stayed in Tony Mayer's divine house there, with a matchless view over the mountains and scented air brought by every breeze. I was passing nearby on my way to somewhere else and suggested I might call in and say hello. Tony said I should stay overnight. This is worth recalling now for the last example of his bovine meanness. When I arrived, and was welcomed with the proper degree of warmth as befitted a guest who was not quite from the top-drawer, I was shown to my sleeping-quarters. In the vaulted stone cellar lay a mattress, directly in the middle of the floor, with a sheet and blanket upon it. No other stick of furniture in the room, no sign of a bedstead. The mattress must have been carried down from somewhere else and placed there for my benefit. I was meant to understand that the whole house was full, and that I should be grateful to have any accommodation at all since I had invited myself. There was some vestige of justification in this, and it would have been churlish, even ill-mannered to protest, but I doubt whether there were no fully-furnished bedrooms available in that magnificent house.

It was one of the most miserable nights I have ever spent. It is nobody's fault that I am especially squeamish about creepy-crawlies, and arachnophobia might have been a disease invented to torment me. I would spend an hour trying to remove a spider from a bathtub into its own safe world rather than kill it, but I would not share a room with it. In my dark cellar (yes, I forgot to mention, it was lit by one naked light-bulb which I had to get out of bed to turn off) there must have been scores of the little black things lurking in cracks and behind stones waiting for the coast to be clear, and with a mattress directly on the floor there was no way I could protect myself from their crawling over it. I had to rely on their better preference for avoiding me. But what if they did not know I was there? Thoughts like these assailed me for up to two hours, and when I turned the light on to investigate, I saw them all scurrying away. Worse still, the light drew the attention of huge hairy moths. If there is anything I hold in greater fear than spiders, it is probably moths, with their pointless directionless flapping and fluttering. I was certain they, in their stupidity, would bump into me, for they lack that sense of choice and discretion which even spiders possess. I think I managed a few snatches of sleep that night by hiding myself entirely beneath the blanket and coming up for air from time to time. Nevertheless, I found a few squashed moths on my pillowcase in the morning.

Tolerating Tony was a lesson in proportions, one which I seemed to have picked up by osmosis, for I had no guide in the subtleties of social intercourse. To some extent, of course, my acquiescence in his behaviour grew out of timidity; I was afraid to contradict, still less chastise, a man so much my senior in age and experience, and with a certain august position withal. But more than that was the feeling, nurtured since my early years with that charming curmudgeon Gilbert Harding (about which I have already written extensively), that no person is defined by a single characteristic against which all other considerations evaporate. Human personality is ever complex and diffuse, now one quality in the ascendant, now another, sometimes reprehensible, sometimes delightful, often both at the same time or within the same hour. Tony Mayer may have had his Scrooge-like component, but he was also interesting, widely-read, passionate about music, able to enjoy a laugh at his own expense, keen to encourage the young, and ever-so-slightly lonely. He and Thérèse were childless, and I had the impression their marriage had been a kind of bargain, a dynastic arrangement, fuelled by respect but little real affection. Social climbing and the cultivation of acquaintance were perhaps his substitutes for love. He may even have been homosexual, but if so, then this was one characteristic he kept firmly hidden. He was, after all, from the generation which regarded such afflictions as unmentionable.

Even then, however, there was one trait of personality which I could not abide in anyone, whatever other wonderful compensations may have lain in waiting, and that was the wilful insulting of inferiors who, by reason not of their rank but of their employment in service, could not possibly defend themselves. This possibly derived from a deeply-buried memory that my mother had herself been a scullery-maid, dependent upon the good nature of those she served, or from an even more stifled notion that I belonged in that station myself. Whatever the reason, I always identified with the underdog, never with the exploiter. There are many, I discovered, who not only identify with the exploiter as a matter of habit, but cannot conceive of doing anything else. In their way, these people are as numb and ignorant as the pub philosophers who think everyone with a title must be stupid.

I was invited to lunch at the Connaught Hotel one Saturday in 1970. It was my first visit to this legendary establishment, and I counted myself extremely fortunate to be included. It was not a place I should ever have set foot in alone, both because I could not have afforded to, and because I should have felt out of place, as it were. The host was Lady Annabel Birley (later Goldsmith), daughter of the 8th Marquess of Londonderry and wife of Mark Birley, founder of the ultra-fashionable nightclub in Berkeley Square which bore his wife's name. (It is still there.) Other guests included her brother, the current Marquess (through whom I came to know the family), two or three others I cannot recall, and a certain Geoffrey Keating.

Now, I knew nothing of this Mr Keating, except that he was much liked by the raffish aristocracy – the sort that throw Sèvres china plates at the wall for fun, or make funny faces behind people's backs, the immature lot who think that bread rolls are meant to hurl across a room, just as one did in school. I believe Keating was a businessman of sorts, a kind of go-between with rich Arab oil sheikhs and their craven American customers, an oiler of wheels, a maker of deals. (He was also, by the way, a fine photographer.) As such, he was valuable to both sides, explaining one to the other, and at ease in different cultures at least on the surface (deep down, I suspect he held all Arabs in contempt). He had no doubt become wealthy leading this kind of life, and the Connaught, to him, was no more impressive than a cafeteria. It was obvious that he would make everyone understand that the only impressive person-age present was himself, and he would do this by keeping his companions amused with silly little stories about his adventures and so-called insights, and especially by demonstrating that he knew how to treat servants. It did not help that he was very quickly drunk, and I had heard that he was almost perpetually sozzled. He died long ago, or I should not dare to write all this.

The waiter took our orders, and we went on talking, or more to the point, listening, for Geoffrey Keating was holding court with selfish determination to give way to no one. There must surely have been a heavy peppering of fear in his make-up, for he fed on attention like a man starved, as if he would crumble as soon as the attention ceased. When the dishes arrived, Keating erupted into the most splenetic, disgraceful, exhibitionistic paddy I have ever seen. Turning on the hapless waiter, he said, 'You bloody fool, that is NOT what I ordered. Where the fuck did you learn to wait at table? Are you deaf or a cretin or what? Now take this foul muck back and bring me what I asked for, and you had better call the manager over as well, perhaps he can teach you a thing or two if it's not too late, or get you another job somewhere, somewhere they don't speak English, because you obviously can't.' The outburst went on longer and louder than these words can portray, the other tables all aware of the rumpus. The poor waiter apologised profusely, metaphorically licking boots and abasing himself, and the manager was soon there to show how obsequious one must be in the presence of a displeased customer. Keating was not easily quietened, and the other people at our table were pleasantly amused at our Geoffrey having one of his tantrums. None was embarrassed. Nobody spared a single thought for the waiter, who at the very least anticipated an almighty reprimand from his employers, perhaps even dismissal, and trembled at having been the cause of such uproar in such a sedate English environment. Especially since none of it was deserved.

I had heard the order Keating had given for his food, and

made a mental note because I wanted to see what it looked like when it arrived (it bore some fancy name in menu-speak which I cannot remember), so I knew that the waiter had indeed brought what was ordered, and that Keating, whether knowingly or not, was wrong. The injustice of it, together with Keating's disgusting arrogance, made a knot in my stomach which no polite smiles could assuage. I found my courage.

I did not look at the offender, still less speak to him, but I felt I had to speak to Annabel. 'Either that man apologises for his conduct, in the presence of us all, or I shall leave,' I said. This, naturally was met with scoffing and smoothing, of the sort one reserves for a disgruntled child. It was apparent within seconds that Annabel would say nothing and that Keating would be humoured. So I got up from the table and left, without the lunch to which I had been looking forward as to a rare treat. I have no idea what was said among them, nor did I ever encounter 'that man' again, but I did not regret my action, however petulant it may have appeared. I seethed with resentment on behalf of the waiter as I walked along Mount Street afterwards, and developed a burning detestation of Keating and his kind. So I did once use my voice.

It is a tribute to the solidity of these people's self-assurance that Annabel did not hold the incident against me, nor even once allude to it. She probably thought I was being silly, and attributed immaturity to my upbringing. She was (and is) a woman of remarkable resilience, much tried and much wounded, but never so bowed by her burdens as to drop one centimetre below the level at which all Vane-Tempest-Stewarts belonged by ancestral right.

There is a portrait of Theresa, Marchioness of Londonderry, Annabel's great-grandmother, by Sargent, which used to hang at Wynyard, the Tempest pile in County Durham, and is now at Alastair Londonderry's more manageable home in Dorset.

Theresa was a Talbot, daughter of the Earl of Shrewsbury, and she brought into the Vane-Tempest-Stewart family a strain of regal *hauteur* born of centuries of deference which surpassed even their sense of place. The Londonderrys, after all, had been among the top half-dozen richest families of Victorian England, their wealth derived from the vast coal-mines on their property. But they had not been austere. Theresa changed that, and the portrait tells you how. Whereas the expression 'looking down your nose' at somebody was always thought, by me at least, to be metaphorical, with Marchioness Theresa it is literal. The painter appears to have been on his knees looking up at her, for the arrogant half-sideways glance is most definitely down the nose to a recumbent observer. I have never seen such a powerfully admonishing portrait. One surely would not have dared speak without first being addressed by her. When she went to see estate workers who were bedridden with illness, she made certain she appeared with all the jewels and furs and fabulous raiment and sparkling tiara that her rank permitted. She said, no doubt truthfully, that the workers appreciated the effort she made, and it cheered them up to see Her Ladyship in full flush as she should be. Yet I wonder whether there was not also an element of demonstration in this, a statement that *she* was the one who had the right to impress in this manner, and nobody else. One cannot imagine her throwing on an overcoat and bonnet to visit the sick. She would have looked absurd.

Well, of all the family Annabel is the one who most resembles her, not, I must emphasise, in manner, for those airs do not belong to our age, but in appearance. She has exactly the same face and, at times, the same ability to overwhelm with a glance. Perhaps she does not realise it, for I have only seen her within the family, as a chattering, attentive mother, fussing around everyone at the huge kitchen-table where family meals always took place (the dining-room reserved for formal occasions), asking endless questions and never heeding the answers. Annabel's talk was a constant stream, her next thought edging in to her head before she had finished giving expression to the first one, and the third hovering in reserve, so that there was simply no time to listen to anyone else. Conversation was impossible; one was audience to a monologue. I assume she must have supplied her own answers, which were always more satisfactory than the ones she might have heard.

She was a kindly woman withal, not given to rancour or malice, but guilty of the innocent tease, at which she thought herself a mistress. She had little idea that her supposedly clever mockery of other people while they were actually in the room was as transparent as a child's (and therefore more forgivable). I think her habit of teasing was a faint echo of Theresa's habit of display, a kind of assertion of right – that she was the one to tease and not to be teased – but it was also, as are so many apparently meaningless and innocent human characteristics, a defence against intimacy. For Annabel had been so unhappy so often that to allow any of that to be seen would have been a dereliction of duty to her family and her rank. She chatted away and made empty fun of people in order not to be known by them.

Annabel's parents died when she was a very young woman, her mother of cancer of the jaw, her father of alcohol (though she was not as young as her brother Alastair, who became Marquess at the age of seventeen and was married within two years). Her marriage to Mark Birley brought her three children – Rupert, India Jane and Robin – and en deuxième noces to Jimmy Goldsmith three more – Zac, Jemima and Ben. Mark was hugely patrician and suited her well. They might have started a country together and installed themselves as regents. As it was, they dominated high-class London night-life in the 1960s with their club Annabel's.

I knew the children when they were still quite young, pre-teenage, for I gave them private lessons in French. The eldest, Rupert, grew into one of the most astonishingly handsome young men I have ever seen – blond waves of hair, blue eyes, perfect proportions, and on top of all this a bright scholar and a charmer not to be beaten. He excelled in every endeavour he attempted, the most remarkable of which was to become fluent in Russian at a time, the Communist era, when few young men with his opportunities would have spent energy learning the language of 'the enemy'. He could, after all, have done very little and led a fine life nevertheless. But Rupert was an achiever, for his own sake, not for anyone else's, and he could not have dawdled and dribbled his way through life.

One day he went for a swim off the coast of Africa and never came back. All kinds of theories were spawned, including suicide, kidnap, and espionage. The fact that he was well-connected and fluent in Russian made one wonder whether he had not been a secret agent for the Russians, sharing the Communist ideal unsuspected by anyone, and had disappeared at a pre-ordained moment to go 'home' to them. It was far-fetched, but not impossible. But he would by now have surfaced, with the end of the Cold War, and been welcomed back. Suicide? There was no reason, but then the reason is frequently so well hidden that suicide is the only way of keeping it secret. It seemed unlikely. Rupert was a strong swimmer. No ransom was ever demanded, no body was ever washed up. He simply stopped being.

It was a devastating blow for Annabel, who needed all her reserves of resilience to survive. A few years before something almost as dreadful had happened to her second son Robin. The maverick gambler and zoo-owner John Aspinall was a family friend (I was much later to write his biography), and they would sometimes spend a weekend at Howletts, the lovely small country house near Canterbury which Aspinall had bought with the winnings from a horse-race and where he was busy establishing the most revolutionary private zoo in the world. One of his primary tenets was that trust between species was not only easy, but desirable, and that threatened species who had never bred in captivity, waiting for a distant death as they sat on concrete slabs eating manufactured food, would soon change their attitude if they were given a nice place to live and good friends to live with. We would often go out for walks in the grounds after tea with a family of gorillas in our wake. Highland gorillas had never bred in a zoo before, but soon Aspinall had dozens of them, and his methods were being applied by serious national zoos which had formerly dismissed him as a playboy. Another of his species was the rare Asian tiger.

Aspinall would walk into the tiger enclosure (several acres of it) at least twice a day to pay a visit, and the magnificent beasts would purr and preen themselves, rubbing against his legs or jumping playfully on his back. One could not resist the conclusion that they enjoyed his visits, and were prepared to share their lives with him, even when they had cubs, picking them up and dumping them in his lap for babysitting. Occasionally friends would go into the enclosure with him. It was always a warm privilege so to do. Annabel accompanied him one day with Robin, then aged about twelve. A perfectly docile tiger, perhaps not knowing what a human being of such small height represented, put her huge paws on his shoulder and ripped his face apart. Robin's lower jaw was hanging off when he was rushed to hospital, and over the next few years he underwent many operations in an attempt to repair the damage. To this day he still bears the marks, understandably, one side of his face not growing at the same rate as the other, but he never bore ill-will against Aspinall, a man whom he continued to admire into adulthood, whose values he cherished, whose achievements he applauded, and whose friendship remained dear.

Annabel's second marriage to the irascible, vain, powerful, and restless Jimmy Goldsmith brought her more trouble. (Jimmy simply could not sit still, but forever paced the room as he talked, as if to lubricate thought.) I was not close to them at this time, but it was no secret that he was cruel to her, often in a physical way, and I suspect he was misogynistic at bottom (as well as being a lustful partner and charming companion to any woman – the two things are not mutually exclusive). Annabel's own memoir of her life has now been published and she deals with her marriage obliquely. I should have welcomed more introspection, because two such dominant people sharing a life together must surely offer some insight into the human capacity for survival. And Annabel is a survivor above all.

Not many years ago she was on a flight bound for Kenya, with most of her family around her, when the pilot was overcome by force and the aircraft went into a headlong dive towards disaster. For many long minutes all passengers thought they were going to die. Annabel wrote to me and said that the utmost horror going through her mind at that time was that her children and grandchildren were going to die with her. That indeed must be the ultimate insult to maternity, that death should negate all you have done for your offspring, before your very eyes. The pilot did regain control, and all ended well, but I felt for the first time that Annabel was vulnerable, and prepared at last to reveal emotion without shame.

Her most innocent weakness was a fondness for royalty, another echo of great-grandmama perhaps, and she would often have the Princess of Wales round for Sunday lunch in the kitchen, with the two young princes, to the extent that she became something of a confidante to the Princess. (To my consternation, I was told to turn up whenever I liked, any Sunday would do, and I never had the time!) In truth, the royals craved Annabel's company rather more assiduously than she sought theirs, a particular friend being Princess Michael of Kent (who the Queen was supposed to have said was 'too grand for the likes of us').

Her elder sister Jane, in contrast, never did seek out royalty, despite having been one of the six ladies-in-waiting who carried the Queen's train at her coronation in 1953. Beautiful and alluring (even in old age), she married Sir Max Rayne and thenceforth led the life, if one may say so without irony, of a housewife (albeit one with servants), devoting energies to family rather than society and accepting her destiny to entertain on the grand scale only when it suited her. She was approachable, giggly, delightful, made up for her sister Annabel's deafness to interlocutors by listening carefully and attentively to everyone, and would have made a superb diplomat. Indeed, that is probably what she became, in an unofficial way, when Max was Chairman of the Board at the National Theatre. But she would do so for his sake, not for her own, since she did not seek attention at all. Which is why, probably, she did it all with such aplomb and success. She was without ambition and without guile. She was simply a fine and dutiful wife, which sounds dull but is in fact one of life's most precious accomplishments. Max was uncomfortably ill for the last years of his life and had to be tended daily, hourly even, as his ability to care for himself evaporated. During all that time it was not servants or nurses who looked after his every need, but Jane herself. Though the effort wore her out, it would never have occurred to her to do otherwise.

Which brings me, not by an imaginative leap, but by a firmly logical step, to another character whom I got to know so well in our middle age that he became a most unexpected, and most undefinable, good friend. I have said that Jane did not entertain on a lavish scale in the tradition of indefatigable society hostesses like Lady Cunard and Lady Colefax of a previous generation, but she did give one huge luncheon party every year about three weeks before Christmas for the entire Vane-Tempest-Stewart clan. Including all manner of cousins stretching by distant threads to the same ascent, they grew to number up to sixty lunch-guests, at round tables in various rooms throughout the ample Rayne residence in Hampstead. Jane made only one rule for attendance, and that was that everybody had to be a member of the family – no strangers. She made one exception for me one year when I asked (typically) to be included, but the other exception she made every year for three decades for a man she always considered to be an 'honorary' member of the family, although he had no blood connection whatever. This was Claus von Bülow.

The name now suggests one thing only, that this was the person tried for the attempted murder of his wife by injection with insulin. More even than that, it would suggest to most people who do not bother to enquire beyond headlines, that he got away with it. The two sensational trials in New York in the 1980s, at the first of which he was found guilty and at the second acquitted on incontrovertible evidence which should have been presented much earlier, made his name front-page news the world over, and he did little to mitigate the effects of this notoriety. He made one huge error in posing for a front-page *Vanity Fair* portrait with his mistress when he ought more properly to have been modestly obscure, and often made jokes at his own expense when everyone else was trying desperately to avoid the subject. This alone indicates that his character might be baffling in its complexity.

The story, briefly, was this. Claus was a playboy and opportunist who hankered after high society and wealth, married a very rich and beautiful woman who thereafter ruined her life and his with drink and drugs, and tried to get rid of her in an undetectable way by injecting her with insulin and waiting for her to die slowly in bed beside him, purposefully delaying the call for an ambulance as she sank into a coma. Such was the portrait depicted in the film *Reversal of Fortune* based upon lawyer Alan Dershovitz's book on the trials, in which Claus was played with sardonic relish and unattractive arrogance by Jeremy Irons. Such, too, was the general view of the man propping up the bar in the local pub.

The truth, even more briefly, was that scientific examination demonstrated there was no insulin in Sunny von Bülow's blood, so that not only did Claus not attempt to kill her, but nobody did. This evidence had been kept out of the first trial, as had the fact that she had tried to kill herself with over a hundred aspirin tablets weeks before and been rescued by hospital intervention. The case against Claus had been con-trived, in perfect American fashion imitating Hollywood (which gradually had more hold over American thought than boring reality), by the suspicions of Sunny's children by her earlier marriage, the von Auerspergs.

As for the man at the centre of this maelstrom, nobody outside his small circle of friends knew him at all. To the world at large he was a sinister manipulator. To his chums, he was quite another person altogether.

Claus had known Jane Rayne since she was a young woman, for the person who had helped him escape from Nazi-occupied Denmark at the age of sixteen was a friend of her uncle's. Thus her connection with him had nothing whatever to do with wives in comas. Claus was Danish by birth, his detractors claiming that he added the aristocratic 'von' to his name in an attempt to sound grander than he was (not true – it was bestowed by Danish royal decree), son of a prominent Danish playwright accused of collaborating with the Nazis. In fact, papa merely wanted to be left alone to write his plays and enjoy his wine, but the reputation stuck, just as it was later to stick far more outrageously to his son. After his escape, the young Claus somehow or other got himself to Cambridge, where he graduated in law at an absurdly young age and practised for eleven years in the chambers of Lord Hailsham. When I knew him years later, there on his desk, in pride of place never to be removed, was his lawyer's horse-hair wig.

He took a position working for the oil billionaire Paul Getty which suited him as no other could have. Getty hated flying, and needed a spokesman to jet around the world as his representative coping with all the negotiations laid down by him at ground-level in Surrey. This enabled Claus to continue in the raffish world of glamorous women and gamblers, expensive dinners and superb wines, wherein he shone. He became one of the set floating around John Aspinall and Jimmy Goldsmith, was amusing company with a ready flow of anecdote and wit, and charmed ladies off their perch with his elegant manners, tall frame, suave voice, and barely concealed lust. He was a popular figure in that world, and quite out of place in any other. Then he met the ravishingly pretty Sunny, and the rest is history. Their daughter Cosima is as gorgeous as her mother was then, and remains, by the way, totally committed to her father, whose honesty she has never doubted.

What made Claus intriguing, at least to me, was the element of playacting in his performance. Yes, he fitted the role beautifully, but I could never rid myself of the impression that it was assumed to some extent, that he had schooled himself into it. He was much deeper and brighter than the role allowed, being fluent in Danish, French, Italian, German and English, and astonishingly well read in the literature of all those languages, but he knew that if he were to display his erudition in the circles wherein he moved, he would be viewed with suspicion, for a certain Philistinism was a required part of the uniform. So he kept quiet, and joked about silly things. Gossip was more productive than music, so gossip prevailed.

One longed to know what he had been like at the age of sixteen, before all these accretions of worldly performance began to adhere. I am sure he had himself forgotten, and preferred the polished persona he had adopted. That it did not quite work (though very nearly) to perfection was demonstrated by his faint lack of tact and discreet proportion. He spoke like an aristocrat and behaved with swish decency towards those of a lower order, but a real aristocrat would not have needed so to do; it would have been so natural as to be invisible. And all those jokes against himself were intended to show that he did not take himself seriously and that he was man enough to rise above reputation, whereas they showed, on the contrary, that he had a fierce need to be seen and acknowledged, and that he fundamentally lacked the wisdom to move quietly into the shadows.

Claus and I first met through Aspinall long before the trials, but we became firm friends after I had written about them. He obviously cherished those who believed in his innocence (not that he was not better off without Sunny and the vapid life she led in Newport, Rhode Island, where his intellectual juices ran dry), for there had been times when he wondered if anybody really did so believe. Some old friends turned cold towards him. But one who never did, who would not even allow herself to think such nonsense for a moment, was Jane. And Jane was such a fine judge of character and nuance, without ever boasting of it, that one knew she was right. It was therefore Claus's greatest badge of honour that he was a family member at the annual lunch for the Vane-Tempest-Stewarts, and I suspect it was his best evidence (save for his daughter Cosima) of unconditional love.

Court orders prevented Claus von Bülow from publishing his own account of the trials and the events which preceded them, otherwise one might have been treated to a valuable first-hand account of a grim tragedy written by a man with legal training, precision of language and delight in style. (Afterwards, he settled in London and became a witty and perceptive theatre critic who positively relished his job.) But worry about his reputation never entirely deserted him. Joking about it was a way of introducing the subject, to give him, or more subtly others around him, a chance to refute the persistent doubts. And he quietly set about checking up on what kind of obituary notices might be in preparation as he passed the age of seventy-five.

Jane and Annabel were in their quite different ways reminders of a vanished age and style, that aristocratic high-point of cultural dominance which was obliterated by 1914. Annabel carried *hauteur* into the modern age, Jane brought the effortless charm of the privileged. Oddly enough, the head of the family, their brother Alastair Londonderry, swept gustily into the modern world while dusting off the remnants of privilege which stuck to him. Lacking the confidence of his sisters, he wanted to make his own way on merit and hard work, with scarcely a nod to his titles. I have written extensively about him in another book, and must resist repetition, but I did on various occasions meet other survivors of that distant world whose memories and manners went back further still. When I was researching for my book on *Great Hostesses*, I came across the fact that the garrulous, generous and gormless American hostess Laura Corrigan on arrival in London had taken the lease of a house in Grosvenor Street which belonged to King Edward VII's mistress, Mrs Keppel, offering twice the expected rent and throwing in a bonus for the Guest Book with which to launch herself into society. Mrs Keppel had two daughters – Violet

Trefusis, whom I had met at her hill-top villa in Florence many years before and found to be irretrievably dotty, and Sonia Cubitt who was still alive and quite ready to see me.

We met the first time at Claridge's, an environment so natural to her that the hotel might have been built on purpose to surround her. She had not much to say about Laura Corrigan, but little matter, for she was herself history, walking, standing, speaking, using circumlocutions, glancing, bowing, all in a nineteenth-century manner which so besotted those around her that the staff at Claridge's themselves reverted to the behaviour of nineteenth-century retainers in response. We had tea before a piano. She wore a hat and gloves. She talked about her mother and the King and about that world before the First World War wherein she fitted; but she was by no means bereft without it, for she carried on as if nothing had really changed. It was both enchantment and instruction to listen to her and feel the soft feather touch and piquant smells of that virtual world brush against one. This kind of history is so evanescent that the new passion for oral testimony kept in archives to enable future generations to leap across the centuries will one day be seen as imperishable. My own bit of oral history was sitting next to me sipping tea in a masterly fashion.

The style has dissipated in Sonia's own granddaughters: Annabel Elliot is the giggly, sportingly chummy friend with whom I spent an uproarious holiday in Italy (with four others, including her future husband Simon Elliot), whereas Camilla Parker-Bowles became familiar in name to every Briton and is now, as Duchess of Cornwall, a hugely steady down-to-earth influence upon her husband the Prince of Wales.

HRH Princess Alice, Countess of Athlone, was in my time the only surviving granddaughter of Queen Victoria. Herself well into her nineties by then, she would, with a little prompting, recall images of her grandmother which made the legendary figure actually audible. We met regularly in a small terraced house in Belgravia belonging to the travel agent Peter Lubbock, half-brother to Peggy Wakehurst, Kay Elliott and therefore, way back, Margot Asquith. He had made a corner for himself getting flights and hotels for the old aristocracy, in which endeavour he had no competition. Princess Alice was one of his most loyal friends, always seated in a corner of the room in order that people should be brought up and presented to her, and not the other way round, and also, I imagine, to prevent anyone from being behind her. As a noisy eighteen-year-old, she said, she had dined at Windsor with the rest of the Royal Family, all keeping quiet and respectful in the Queen's presence, never speaking unless spoken to, with long silences broken only by the clatter of cutlery. Being young and enthusiastic she found this all too trying, and would frequently whisper a funny remark to one of her neighbours. Even this did not escape Victoria's attention, however. In suitably imperious accent, at the far end of the table, she declared, 'Moderate your tones, my dear.' Alice could still remember how she trembled at the admonishment.

I have heard it said, by people who see her almost daily, that Queen Elizabeth II is in reality a very modest person who is often taken aback by public expressions of affection. One must surely make a distinction here between Elizabeth the woman, who may well indeed be modest, and Elizabeth the Queen, to whom complete and utter deference is as ordinary as a glass of water (servants must still dart behind a door and remain invisible if they see her walking down a corridor at Buckingham Palace). Reliable snapshots of her in an unguarded moment are extremely rare, and prized precisely because they humanise the otherwise august personage. When I wrote a very foolish book called *Dreams About Her Majesty The Queen*, based upon the assumption that everyone in Britain must dream about her at some stage or another and collecting some robustly ludicrous examples (including my own recurrent nightmare of being invited to dine at the Palace, forgetting to put on any clothes at all, and conducting strained conversation while covering my nakedness with a napkin), the Palace ordered half a dozen copies. I later heard from a visitor that the Queen had found an excuse to allude to one of them with a sly jerk of the finger and the remark, 'Have you seen this frightfully funny book about *me*?' The suggestion of shyness is bewitching.

On another occasion the Queen was with her sister Princess Margaret at the Royal Opera House, as private individuals, not on a state occasion. Between them sat the dancer and later Director of the Royal Ballet, Anthony Dowell. At one point the Queen's attention to what was happening on stage slackened. Margaret leant across and shook her arm. 'Lilibet, Lilibet,' she said, 'do wake up!' Ah, the ubiquity of human weakness! How reassuring.

CHAPTER SEVEN

Writers

The theatre is of necessity a gregarious profession, and a roomful of actors will quickly discover that each one has worked with several of the others at some time or another, making a web of interconnections which feels like an extended family. They do not all become close friends, of course, but they do all know one another to a greater or lesser degree.

It is not thus with writers, again for obvious reasons. With exception made for journalists, who report sometimes to the same office, and consult one another daily to swap information, contacts and ideas, the creative writer must work in solitude or he cannot work at all. His day must be uncluttered, his attention unsought by any intruder. Also, writers tend not to consult among themselves, but produce work which is undimmed by influence, which often leads to two people devoting three years to the same task and publishing books on the same subject within the same month, to the consternation of both. The result of all this is that writers do not meet, congregate or confer (except on committees, like PEN or the Society of Authors), and are often strangers to each other. I say this because the layman assumes, naturally I suppose, that writers form a kind of club, whereas in reality they are islands to themselves, and when they do meet they invariably talk about money and figures rather than the muse and the method. It was not until I had been writing for twenty years that I dared consider myself an author, and then only tentatively, still shy of admitting as much in the presence of a 'real' one. So the researcher of the future will look fruitlessly to authors for intimate revelations of other authors; instead, he will find what he wants in the reminiscences of 'ordinary' people – wives, husbands, neighbours, greengrocers and men-friends.

Francis King is a splendid exception which proves the rule. His memoirs are a feast of accurate portraits of contemporary literary figures, told with verve and an immediacy which makes them vivid on the page. He knew them all well for the very reason stated above, that he met them at committees (he sat on more than a handful all of his life) and developed friendships with them by dint of frequent collision. I sat on one committee only, and the people there were known to me already by accident or chance encounter, not because we were writers.

Most of them I met in a doctor's surgery. Well, not quite, but at the doctor's dinner-table after a consultation in the surgery. The doctor in question was the notoriously well-connected Patrick Woodcock, general practitioner to actors, painters and writers of the day, to whom he would dispense whatever medicine they craved and whatever comforting wisdom he could invent, providing they would stay for dinner. For Patrick was a far better cook than he was a doctor, effortlessly producing good simple meals as if by snapping his fingers, for he never seemed to be absent when entertaining his friends. He was a perfect exemplar of that *geltungsbedürfnis* which informed the relentless climb of Sybil Colefax up the social ladder between the wars – that is the need to absorb worth from the celebrity of others, and the ability to say bland things which appear to be the result of deep cogitation. In fact, he never said anything of any moment, and contrived to tell his interlocutor what that person wanted to hear, precisely because it reflected his own opinion. Patrick's instincts were sharp, his social success paramount in London, and there was a time when I am sure a letter addressed to Patrick Woodcock, London, would have found its way easily to his house in Tachbrook Street.

But a dinner at Patrick's house was always an occasion, and the company always an excitement. It was there that I met Angus Wilson, Margaret Lane, David Hockney, Patrick Procktor, Stephen Spender, Christopher Isherwood and Rosamund Lehmann. My acquaintance with them all survived, much to Patrick's delight, for he had no jealousy, but wanted to see his friends get on well together. There is one writer whom I knew better than any other, namely Beryl Bainbridge, but I did not meet her with Patrick. As I have told elsewhere, we met because I knocked one day on her front door, and we fell into one another's arms immediately. She was, come to think of it, of a later generation, perhaps ascending towards renown when Patrick was preparing for retirement. So my impressions of those writers who were Patrick's guests are episodic and fragmentary, rather than the issue of long and intimate connection.

Rosamund Lehmann was a figure of the past when I knew her. *Dusty Answer* was firmly established in the canon of English Literature, but no longer created the noise and fuss it had done when first published. I rather felt that Rosamund resented her descent into the role of has-been, and it was therefore especially heartening that all her books were reissued by Virago before she died, and she was able to taste the delight of being rediscovered by a new generation. But around 1967 she was still sunk in neglect, and it showed. She had allowed herself to spread like a blancmange, or a large melting cream-cake, dolloped into a wide armchair and likely to have to be scooped out with a spoon. Her legs apart, the edge of her knickers showing, she hardly seemed the stuff of legend, and yet one did not have to look far to see that she had once been a ravishing beauty, and when Selina Hastings's biography came out in 2002 there indeed, on front and back covers of the jacket, were pictures of Rosamund when young which would make any man long to be swamped by her love. She still had sexual allure, an enticement and warmth concealed behind those lovely eyes, peeking above the fat of the rosy cheeks, and even her bloated body retained its hint of welcome.

Not that sex ever entered into the conversation. All Rosamund would talk about in those days was 'spiritualism', by which she meant her virtual daily contact with the beyond. This was a state of mind and of emotion quite out of keeping with her previously shrewd intelligence, but rendered necessary to her, implacably essential, by tragedy. She had never recovered from the early death of her daughter, and fancied she was still able to be with her, to listen to her, to interpret her wishes and regrets, by spiritual means. This had been going on for years, and we all thought her quite dotty, but there was no mistaking her earnestness and belief. She did not need to pretend; because she *thought* she was in contact with the world of the spirit, then in a sense she *was*. It is all told with great generosity as well as honesty by Selina. Rosamund had longed for the biography to be published in her lifetime, for she was markedly vain, and not without reason. But Selina, accurately feeling the tension which precedes a movement of the earth, and knowing that her subject would interfere with every page, wisely set the project aside and got on merrily with her work on Evelyn Waugh instead.

Angus Wilson also became a has-been in his lifetime, which was sad, for he was not vain and only minded professionally. Rather than thinking the world had turned its back on him, he wondered whether his work had been worth the extraordinary notice it had won in the first place. It was not nice to watch a man pushed into self-doubt by fickle public taste. Angus had risen from behind a desk at the British Museum to become England's most renowned post-war novelist. He could do no wrong. His books were applauded and analysed by critics, lapped up by readers, and all sold extremely well. I sometimes felt they were too dense and complex for me, what one used to call 'too clever by half ', but clever they certainly were, plot and character overlapping and feeding one another in the hands of a master craftsman who knew what he was doing on page 1 and had already decided what he was going to do on page 300.

Angus came to dinner at my house in Caithness Road a number of times, and was reliably entertaining, with his high-pitched mousy voice and twinkling teasing demeanour. He was always kind towards and curious about other people (the sign of a great novelist, or one of the signs anyway) and never keen to spin his own web, whereas Rosamund was busy spinning hers even when you did not notice. At this time I believe I had written nothing of note, and quizzed him (rather pretentiously I suppose) on the quarrel between Sartre and Mauriac about whether one could control one's characters once they had been created. (Sartre had accused Mauriac of being a puppeteer, whereas his, Sartre's, characters were left free to make their own decisions; to which Mauriac had more or less said, 'Poppycock.') Angus took Mauriac's side, and confessed that he sometimes wondered whether his characters would have behaved in the way he designated for them, if left alone, but since the experiment could never be made, he would have to go on pulling the strings. It was one of the rare times I have heard a writer talk about his work.

Another was Iris Murdoch, who declared over dinner that she felt her fiction had failed because none of her characters remained in the memory after the book was closed. 'I wish I had been able to create characters that lived on outside the book, as Dickens did,' she said. 'Until you do, you have only written about ideas, in the end, and not about people.' This was a fine self-assessment, for one dug through those busy pages of her novels to find out what they were really *about* (namely Good and Evil), while the people who toiled and squabbled and manoeuvred through her pages, messing up their own and everyone else's lives, did not strike one as true. None of us had ever met anyone who behaved like that, or even spoke like that. They were Iris's people, sprung out of her fervid imagination, and they could not really *be* in the real world. By contrast, all of Dickens's characters are totally real and touchable, from beginning to end, even those whose mannerisms and repeated remarks might be exaggerated. What Dickens did was to exaggerate the truth, but it remained the truth despite the big brush. Iris exaggerated her inventions. True people become part of the reader's own mental baggage, part of their own past. Thus Dickens's astonishing achievement was to kidnap our own memory banks and people them with his memories. Iris was right. She never achieved this.

This conversation took place at dinner in Caithness Road, where she sat at the head of the table as I toiled in the kitchen. Oddly enough, it was always like coming home for her, since by the strangest coincidence she had lived all her childhood in the house opposite, No 12 Caithness Road. She had been born in Dublin, but her parents moved to London when she was an infant, and she stayed in that house until she was about twelve years old, I believe. A few doors up on my side of the road, at No 52, two young actors had shared a one-floor flat in a conversion as they struggled to earn their keep and make their name. They were Richard Pasco and John Osborne. It was in that house that Osborne sat down and wrote *Look Back in Anger*, making frequent reference throughout to the shop at the end of the road where Jimmy Porter sent his put-upon and subservient wife. This shop was Turner's, a local provisions store in Blythe

Road where I went regularly. It later changed hands, and was renamed 'Used-to-be-Turners', the owners patently knowing their theatrical history (*Look Back* was by then overwhelmingly famous). Still later it was bought by Pakistani merchants, who had no idea who John Osborne was. The association and the historical memory have both evaporated.

All of which is by the by. To get back to Iris Murdoch, it has been announced in books by both John Bayley, her widower, and by A N Wilson, her friend, that she was sexually voracious, and the film based on Bayley's book – *Iris* – makes no bones about her appetites in this regard. One is bound to accept that all this happened. But they also suggested that she was sexually alluring. Now one might just see that she could have been rounded, sensual, fleshy, and available, but there was no sign of it remaining when I knew her. She seemed rather to repel any advance by her very appearance and clothing. Dressed in what looked like a tent, with her head poking out of the apex and the body utterly concealed underneath, she was in appearance colourless, even dour. Her hair likewise appeared to have been cut with garden shears. There was no make-up to disguise her kindly motherly face, and she might easily have passed for a tramp who had given herself a bit of a clean-up in order to go out with the nobs.

But if it was with difficulty that one could imagine her appearance arousing male attention, it was perfectly easy to see how her personality might, for she was astonishingly sweet-natured, with a soft Irish brogue and genuine interest in people. She did not show off or dominate conversation; she was mild, receptive, warm, even cosy until you realised you could not cuddle that formidable intellect, and were quite happy to listen instead. John Bayley was also sweet and amenable, given to smiling with his whole face and accepting compliments with child-like deference. He, too, looked as if he had no bathroom mirror, his hair uncombed, white and untamed, and had dressed as if by accident in whatever came to hand. Jowly and bespectacled and wilfully vague, he looked like a character from Dickens himself, without really trying.

The two of them together were unforgettable, a unique, unconventional and entirely fortuitous (it seemed) pairing that worked against all expectations. When I organised the International PEN Congress in 1967 or thereabouts, with delegates from all over the world, I was called upon to ferry them all from a hotel in Cromwell Road to the Banqueting Hall in Whitehall, where the Government was offering a reception. I chartered twenty buses, which were parked all round the hotel at every corner, and as one filled up I sent it on and started with the next. Nineteen of them left. Some delegates having got fed up with waiting took the Underground or a taxi instead, so when the last bus pulled up there were only two people left to get into it. They were Iris Murdoch and John Bayley, who gleefully sat in the front seat, tickled pink to have the whole bus to themselves. It was then that I heard her call him 'Princess', evidently a nickname she used a lot. It could not have been less appropriate, therefore more beguiling.

Judi Dench's portrayal of her in the film was heart-breaking. Judi told me they never met, but her intuition is so fine they didn't need to. She did not attempt to impersonate Iris, and she never has taken such an approach in any of her roles. Her business was to find the truth of a brilliant mind watching itself crumble and disintegrate, to show fear sinking into shapeless indifference. My last sight of Iris was on the station platform at Oxford. We were waiting for different trains. I walked over to greet her. She looked startled and may not have recognised me. I kissed her on both cheeks, having begun before I saw her childish alarm and unable to draw back. We exchanged idiotic remarks and she left. I now realise that the illness must already have started to ravage her head. She either did not know me, or did not know what to do about me. Her abilities to recognise, to respond, and to initiate were muddled, like loose threads hanging from a worn tapestry, connecting to nothing, leading nowhere.

Spender and Isherwood were writers of an earlier generation, coeval with Rosamund's. I knew them separately, and found them so diverse in character and talent that it was impossible to imagine them as part of the famous trio of the thirties (the other being Auden), which I suppose they were only in the confections of literary commentators. Of course they had been friends, and of course they had supported similar political ideals, but they were not like peas in a pod. Spender was very quiet-spoken, almost whispering, and with a gentleman's demeanour and reticence, not wishing to shock or surprise, anxious to be private and discreet. Isherwood, by contrast, was mischievous to say the least, eager to stand out as a renegade and brave individualist, keen on the limelight. There was something remorselessly adolescent about him, whereas Spender was equally determined to be austere and avuncular. Stephen did have his moments of fun, but he kept quiet about them. He confided in me that, unknown to his lovely wife Natasha, he had been conducting a sporadic *amitié* with a man in the United States, but I had the impression that he would rarely speak about such matters, and that he raised the subject with me precisely because he was worried about it; he agonised over the betrayal which it involved, at the same time declaring that nothing would interfere with his deep love for his wife. He was adult and responsible. Isherwood was cheeky and adventurous; he gleefully embraced danger.

I think these disparities of character were reflected in their writing. Isherwood's work as he grew into handsome old age was that of a man saying, 'Look, I'm still here, don't forget me, I can still show you something,' with almost desperate display. Spender's old age disappeared into undemonstrative respectability. He still wrote, but did not draw attention to the fact, and his poetry had a quiet dignity which I think will allow his work to endure, not as masterpieces, but as beautiful contributions to literature. Isherwood's work, flashy and intemperate, is likely to date much more quickly. Yet Isherwood's posthumous fame already eclipses Spender's. The renown of each is in inverse proportion to his worth. In personal company, I enjoyed being with Christopher, but felt honoured to be with Stephen.

When I first met Alan Bennett he was already something of an English (*emphatically not* British) icon, having been one of the four undergraduates who had transformed and rejuvenated satire on stage with their review *Beyond the Fringe* a few years earlier, first at Edinburgh, then in the West End, and finally on Broadway. Jonathan Miller was the egg-head, forbiddingly intellectual and unlikely to indulge in idle chatter, one imagined; Peter Cook and Dudley Moore were gifted adolescents, superbly iconoclastic and cheeky, with wit enough to cope with five hundred bores. But Bennett was the wickedly observant one, reflective, a little sad, piercingly accurate in his gentle mockery of human foibles and miscalculations and malapropisms, the celebrant of English ordinariness in all its unintended hilarity. Mild might describe his humour, but devastating might better describe its effect. His mock-sermon in the show, on the theme 'My brother Esau was an hairy man, but I am a smooth man', had been for me the high point of disabling laughter, which makes me smile in recollection even now, half a century later.

It was not, however, as a performer that I encountered Alan, but as an historian. Having abandoned *Beyond the Fringe*, and the stage with it, he had returned to the academic life, which suited him as if it had been invented to give him comfort, and was a lecturer at Oxford. Low leather armchairs, dusty books, mugs of tea and patched elbows matched his soft, diffident Yorkshire vowels with perfect ease; Mayfair drawing-rooms and Manhattan cocktail parties fitted him as a thimble might fit an elephant's trunk. Alan was doing some research at the Public Record Office, under the guidance of my great friend Kenneth Timings, then Principal Assistant Keeper, so it was as a shuffler among books that Kenneth brought him as an extra guest to his weekly dinner with Cecil Woodham-Smith in Mount Street. I was another guest that evening.

It was immediately clear that Alan combined a potentially crippling shyness with an almost intrusive curiosity. He physically shrank with embarrassment should anyone allude to his theatrical talents, almost coyly nodding his head or throwing his hands up to his face as if he had unwittingly said something offensive; at the same time, he was taking in every word that was said, spotting the lurking humour within an innocent remark, almost fishing for it, as if his very presence provoked it. In a way, that was indeed the case; not that people consciously spoke more allusively or absurdly because he was there, but that he would notice allusions and absurdities which would not have been apparent to anyone else. Alan was the litmus-paper. Occasionally he would quickly scribble something down, and one might very easily find it repeated, even years later, in one of his plays on the West End stage. I remember Cecil talking about having to cross the Atlantic for publicity purposes when her first volume of *Queen Victoria* came out and, having done so by sea, pausing, almost as though scripted, to ask Alan, 'Do you *know* the Atlantic?' Now that is not an intrinsically funny question, it is merely put in an unusual way. To Alan it was hysterical, and on stage in one of his plays it was delightfully odd. This kind of jackdaw picking of pearls will one day prove a source of tremendously indulgent research for somebody attempting an analysis of Alan Bennett's drama (I don't know if anybody has done this already), and I wouldn't be at all surprised if the line he has the Queen deliver in his *A Question of Attribution* was not first heard in a bus queue or somewhere similar: 'I suppose Paradise will be somewhat of a letdown for Us.'

That a man could expose himself nightly on stage, yet off-stage be shrinkingly timid, was an amazement to me. We were once discussing David Hockney, who came from a nearby town in Yorkshire (one is from Leeds, the other from Bradford, and both retained an indomitable accent), and I said I should invite them both to dinner and they could meet and compare reminiscences. Alan was thrown into panic. 'Oh no,' he said, 'I couldn't. I would be far too shy. Oh no, don't ask, I couldn't.' Unless I am an utter fool, and what he really meant was that he didn't want to see me, it all seemed totally genuine to me. We were once involved in an engagement together in the morning, and I proposed that he come to the house for lunch afterwards. When we got there, Brendan Price, one of my lodgers and an up-and-coming actor, was preparing an omelette. 'Oh no,' cried Alan, 'I don't want to be any trouble, really, just give me a biscuit and a cup of tea.' As the years passed, it became a running joke that he would routinely refuse an invitation, on the grounds that he ate nothing (but really because he didn't want to see anyone, or be seen by them), and to his credit he roared with laughter when I told him the story, I trust true, of Tallulah Bankhead, who, pressed to accept an invitation to dine, found excuses to turn down Monday, Tuesday and Wednesday, but when her tormentor suggested Thursday, ultimately gave in, saying, 'Oh fuck it, I'll come on Monday.'

Nevertheless, he was sometimes spotted at Giovanni's off St Martin's Lane dining with Alec Guinness or John Gielgud, presumably for professional purposes people whom he could not refuse, and Giovanni's was a famous refuge for those who did not want to be stared at, being tucked away down an alley which could not be discovered by accident. I used to imagine the relief with which he got back to his cluttered Victorian house and poked his feet back into familiar friendly slippers.

There, in the front garden, was the smelly, obstinate, unreasonable lady in the van, who had parked originally in the road outside and stayed, there and later in the garden, for years, to be immortalised (the verb is not excessive) in his plays and essays. I came across her once or twice. She frightened me. It was instructive that Alan, arguably wary of straightforward people who did not live in layers of unwashed jumpers, was more at ease with a bizarre woman who did, and who moreover dumped her shit in a bag outside the gate. Her eccentricity and his tolerance melted into one, and he was much more at home with her antisocial intransigence than with the polished politenesses of standard social living. He positively celebrated the eccentrics of this world, and used his quiet scalpel to dissect the much more offensive platitudes and presumptions of its self-congratulatory matrons. Other people might be made angry by pomposity; Alan derided it with a whimsical smile. In that, he represented the best of English humour, that which is derived from an affectionate upsetting of the apple-cart, rather than a violent crushing of it.

In my view, Alan Bennett's work will find a place in our literary history as enduring and important as that of Swift, without his ever having had to sharpen the knife. That is a rare achievement.

No writer could offer a sharper contrast than Jessica Mitford, whose knife was perpetually on the hone. Also fiercely observant, but without an ounce of diffidence in her nature, Decca's book *The American Way of Death* was a shriek of sarcasm, defined by a relish in choosing the most wounding word, the most glancing inference. Like her sisters Nancy, Diana and

Deborah, she revered the power of language, its elegance and capacity to persuade, but being more angry than her sisters, her language was correspondingly crisper and more subversive. She delighted in causing the most almighty rumpus.

In this, Decca reflected her own personal history, told many times over in dozens of books by various people, of constant upheaval and rebellion. In person, however, she rarely raised her voice. While being warm and friendly, she retained the burning indignation which had fuelled her from adolescence onwards, and like Bertrand Russell, she remained adolescent in her enthusiasms and idealism. Never once was Decca tempted by the ease of cool, middle-aged indifference. When I wrote a long magazine study of her sister Diana Mosley, whom I knew far better and loved deeply, Decca (who had been estranged from her throughout adulthood) remonstrated with me that I 'had failed to get to the bottom of her'. She thought her sister wicked, and anyone who tried to show otherwise must be flawed. I did not, however, earn her enmity. She merely thought it a pity that I had failed to see the truth. There was a story that Diana had sought some kind of reconciliation when Decca's son, half-Jewish, was due to study at the Sorbonne in Paris. She wrote to her sister suggesting that it would be a 'good idea' if the young man were to visit her and Sir Oswald, whose lovely house Le Temple de la Gloire was only a few miles outside Paris. Nancy mischievously suggested that Decca had replied curtly, 'Better not. We don't want him turned into a lampshade, do we?' The mixture of cruelty, tease and humour was typical of Nancy. Only a future historian will be able to corroborate the story, as the twelve thousand letters between all Mitford sisters have been carefully preserved at Chatsworth; six hundred of them have already been edited and published.*

* The Mitfords, ed. Charlotte Mosley, Fourth Estate, 2007

A writer whom I came to know through my work on criminal cases was Colin Wilson. Like Jessica Mitford, he had started his career with a comet-like blaze of fury, becoming, with *The Outsider*, one of the few writers to make front-page headlines in the daily newspapers on the publication of a book, and probably the only one so to do with a book of philosophy. He was young, reflective and exciting, and came to be grouped with the so-called Angry Young Men whom the press so labelled after John Osborne's hero in *Look Back in Anger*, and who included Kingsley Amis and John Braine as well as Osborne himself. In fact, Colin was only included because his book was published just two weeks after the opening of *Look Back*, but facts were never a worry to newspaper editors, then as now. The rest of them took the opposite route to Decca as they grew old. Amis descended into a spluttering right-wing bully, Braine into middle-class comfort and anonymity, Osborne into calm self-satisfaction. All of these writers could have taken lessons in consistency from Jessica Mitford, firebrand to the end. Colin developed and deepened his philosophical work with a series of books on existentialist themes and many encyclopaedias on crime and the occult,

Colin was wonderfully polite and a kind host, even cosy, with, also, a frank admission of his own exceptional insights. 'Nobody understands the march of philosophy in the novel since Fielding as I do,' he once told me. 'I am the only person who has the mind to see it.' His industry and assiduity were blinding. He worked all day until tea-time, every day, for years on end, producing over one hundred books and countless articles and reviews. His study was in the basement of the house he had bought as a refuge from press attention back in the early sixties, tucked away in the low hills of Cornwall, difficult to find and with directions impossible to remember. He had fled there with his young wife and remained ever since, adding to the property by building ever more barns to house his huge and expanding library. The house itself was a comfy shambles, slightly scruffy, with old sagging furniture, and a lovely log fire round which all life assembled – children, mother-in-law, cats, the lot. Colin was invisible all day, seemingly walled up in his cellar-cum-study, which one approached by going down a bare wooden staircase into the foundations of the house. (It was strictly out-of-bounds; I came across it by accident and without permission.) The cellar was not only lined with books on all four walls, but stuffed with books in piles all over the floor, some reaching to a height of six feet. In the midst of all this sat Colin with typewriter at his tiny desk, all but submerged and flattened by his surroundings. Had all the piles of books simultaneously collapsed, one felt sure Colin would have been buried.

Guests were housed in the barns, where they were likewise looked down upon by books, and in winter warmed only by an electric bar. They would be invited to the house for meals, the most ritualistic of which was at five in the afternoon, when Colin would emerge from his cellar, blink at the light, take a shower, then sit by the fire and consume smoked salmon with a glass of fine white wine, his head hidden within an enormous hair-dryer of the sort seen in hairdressing salons. It was a nicely ridiculous sight, repeated religiously every day, to the humour of which he appeared utterly immune. Like all great men, he cared not a fig for what others might think. For the record, I must say that I enjoyed being with him, for his supply of wine never faltered, and his well-informed conversation, albeit rather self-regarding at times, never bored. He was already an incipient eccentric. Were he to live into his eighties, and enjoy a revival of literary fame, he would surely slide easily into the eccentric role full-time.

An eccentric of an entirely different order was Stephen

Sondheim. Initially known for his collaboration with Leonard Bernstein on *West Side Story*, for which he wrote the lyrics, and subsequently for a string of brilliant Broadway musical shows which issued entirely, music and words, from his own fertile imagination, he gradually mutated, at least in Britain, into a philosophical poet who happened to use Broadway shows as his medium of expression. As such, he was held in enormously high regard by intellectuals, quite apart from and in addition to his appeal to the public, and was for a year a visiting professor of the theatre at Balliol College, Oxford. In an early book I wrote, on the forms and nature of literature (not, alas, published, but great fun to write), I included extracts from Steve's lyrics in order to illustrate the poetic technique of elision. But I quite forget how I met him.

At any rate, it was early on in his career, around 1970 perhaps, for he was still young, though already showing signs of crusty intolerance. Though he wrote wonderful parts for women, I suspect he was secretly something of a misogynist. He was born into affluence, the legacy of which was an elegant ease in any society, and the absence of any hint of embarrassment. Handsome, suave, a magnet for attention, he was fawned upon by ladies, but preferred the company of men. Once when he was on a visit to London, staying of course at the Savoy Hotel, I invited him to dinner with my friend and lodger Chattie Salaman, a teacher at LAMDA and sister-in-law of Alec Guinness. She was the most amiable of souls, soft-spoken and smiling, agreeable, not at all argumentative, interested in people, but Steve took an immediate dislike to her for some reason, and destroyed the dinner by telling her, 'I know your sort, I know the kind of woman you are, a ball-breaker. You smirk and simper, but underneath it all you are bent on under-mining men.' Poor Chattie had said nothing offensive, but she had contributed to intellectual conversation, and displayed, willy-nilly, that she had experience in the theatre. Like a lot of American men who live in a matriarchal society of which they outwardly approve, Sondheim felt threatened by clever women.

He had the grace to telephone the next morning to apologise, but he did not alter his assessment; rather did he repeat it. I made a point of calling him whenever I went to New York, and on one occasion he invited me round for a drink (and proffered a silver cigarette-box which contained up to forty ready-made joints – I suppose he employed someone to roll them for him). He would arrange a ticket for me to his current show, which was a blessing, since they were always sold out. After *Into the Woods* I told him that the show made clear that creating art was a hard slog. 'Thank God somebody has noticed that it's all a question of work, work, work,' he said. 'You'd be amazed how many people assume I do it all as a pastime.' These conversations were on the telephone. I never had more than the one short visit, and I gained the impression that he did indeed work all day long and hated having time wasted on trivia or superficial social chat. The house itself was a brilliant expression of individuality. A rare three-storcy brown-stone townhouse on Manhattan's east side, it was replete with an exhaustive collection of board games, from the early nineteenth-century onwards, in every room and on every shelf, it seemed. Katharine Hepburn lived next door. He offered to get 'Kate' to drive me to Broadway, where she herself was appearing at a neighbouring theatre, but it was not to be. That would have been a story to cherish.

Painters were generally to be found in Patrick Woodcock's white sitting-room above the surgery (white sofas, white cushions, white walls, white fluffy carpet, colour only in flowers in vases and paintings on walls), for he was a notable patron of living artists and assembled an enviable collection. There were more Keith Vaughans in that house than almost anywhere else, I believe, and Patrick had quietly helped Keith to commit suicide as an escape from a vicious terminal cancer. There was also my favourite Hockney lithograph, *Flowers and Vase 1969*, which I frequently hinted would be welcome as a legacy, but it was no use; before Patrick died forty years later he dispersed his collection among friends, and I was not one of the recipients. Both Hockney and Procktor became friends of mine through sharing the same doctor.

Procktor was a strange, refined, effete, serpentine man, tall and very thin, with a reedy voice and languid manner for all the world like a character from an Evelyn Waugh novel; one felt sure he would have been 'in place' had he flourished in the twenties. He pronounced every word with deliberation, as if it were tuning up to be used orchestrally. He was kind and generous, but with an air of divorce from the real world which made it difficult, for me at least, to connect. He always seemed to be thinking about something else, to be only half-present. He married and had a son, which surprised many, and then tragedy flattened him when his house in Manchester Square caught fire and all his paintings perished. Thereafter he turned to drink, and it was pitiful in his last year to find him at the Garrick Club, where he stayed for he was otherwise homeless, slurring his words and being avoided, not because Garrick members are intolerant, far from it, but because Patrick appeared to be in a trance, preferring not to be interrupted. I was one of the few to engage him in conversation at that period, and he fondly remembered me from our youth. There was actually a solid loyalty about him, and I wish I had valued it more than I did. He succeeded in drinking himself to death in 2003.

The most salient characteristic about David Hockney was his shining honesty. He was clever enough to dissemble had he wanted to, so his candour was by no means the result of innocence. He simply did not see the point in giving voice to something other than what was in his mind. It would have been silly, a waste, a nonsense. So he always spoke the truth. This made him a double-edged asset on any radio or television programme, where he was occasionally interviewed for his opinion on this or that. For at first, it was refreshing to have a guest who talked frankly, not in meandering riddles which had then to be interpreted, and his example was blazing when set against that of politicians of whatever party. But it did not take long for the producers to realise that this outstanding talent for truth-telling was an embarrassment; it both made follow-up questions unnecessary, striking the interviewer dumb, and it sold the listener or viewer short (at least in their view) on entertainment. For they wanted conflict and adventure, not disabling candour. So David was not asked as often as he should have been. Over a long career as a public figure, and as one of the two or three most famous living British artists, his amount of air-time must have amounted in proportionate terms to a matter of a few minutes.

On a personal level, the straight reliability of David in conversation was intoxicating. It was a relief to dispense with small talk and the cunning positioning for influence as you tested a subject or a reaction, all of which was redundant with him. Not that he would turn on you with scorn if you attempted it, for he knew well enough the habits of the world, but he would cut through it with such powerful simplicity of manner that you wondered why you had ever attempted it. His emotions were therefore correspondingly equable. I never saw him petulant, or blusteringly angry, or inconsolably sad. He saw what was, and dealt with it. Shortly after he met fellow artist Peter Schlesinger, with whom he fell in love and who was the inspiration for many of his finest paintings of the sixties, he told me he felt extremely lucky. No blather about the man's qualities and goodness or whatever, just the fact. I would not have called him lucky; he got what he deserved, for his hugely unconventional honesty was a terrific magnet. People liked him for it, in a way utterly different from their attraction to other interesting men. He inspired confidence, respect, and affection in equal measure.

Even professionally, he did not appear to resent the intrusion of fools. I was with him in his studio when he was working on the very large canvas *Le Parc des Sources, Vichy 1970*, and told him what I thought of the perspective and the stillness of it, in what must surely have been the vapid mouthings of an outsider. He could have banished me. He could have silenced me. He could have mocked me. But he did none of this, for David Hockney, though famous and courted, was not remotely self-important. He knew what he wanted to do as an artist, and that was between him and himself, but he was not vain or self-satisfied and triumphant. Had one asked him, he would again, I suspect, have said he was 'lucky'. He certainly did in life what he wanted. He painted because it was his passion, every day and for long hours. It was what he enjoyed most in life, and he was lucky enough to be paid a fortune for it. He gave me several proofs of his etchings for the Grimm series, which I treasure and which he signed, merely because I admired them and said so. I did not get my favourite, the boy in the fish, because he could not find one in his studio, but he did spend some time looking for it for me.

David went to live in California, also because he wanted to. He felt that the English distaste for the brashness and dullness of California was mistaken, and to demonstrate, he took me on a three-hour ride in the mountains not far from Hollywood, usually neglected by visitors because they do not go there for scenery and therefore do not expect it. He had three cars, I think, and one of them, a convertible with the most powerful stereo system I have ever encountered, was reserved for this mountain drive. David had fashioned a tape especially for the journey, composed entirely of extracts from Wagner, and so cleverly contrived that, as we turned a corner at the summit of a long hill suddenly to be confronted with a range of peaks hidden beyond, which we (or rather, I) had not suspected during the climb, a blazing crescendo of music exactly matched the moment. He had timed the music to reflect every minute of the journey, three hours of it, like a theatre director whose cast was the mountains he so loved.

It would seem, on the face of it, that Hockney was an eccentric from an early age. To dye one's hair blond, to wear odd socks of violent but contrasting colours, to live in the Hollywood hills and take one's holiday in Bridlington, are not these signs of eccentricity? I think not, emphatically not, because David was never an invented man, a confection to seduce; these were simply things he did, with no concealed intention. He was a plain Bradford boy, who happened to have the talent of a genius, but he retained his heavy accent and his beguiling ordinariness, his mature attitude towards his homosexuality, which was that it was not worth talking about, really, and if other people wanted to, then it was up to them, and his courage in the face of increasing deafness which would ultimately isolate him. But as long as he had his brushes, his occasional dope, and in the latter years his beloved dogs, what could an affliction do to deflate him? He was a shining example, a hero in fact.

By a perverse leap of unlikely connection, Wayne Sleep looms (not too grand a word for a little man, I hope) as another personality gifted with that spark of originality which immediately suggests eccentricity, for the pre-eminent artist and the mercurial ballet-dancer were devoted friends, and Wayne figures in several of David's paintings. There is a fine drawing, issued in a limited edition, which is now quite rare, and an unfinished double-portrait in oils, with George Lawson, belonging to that period when David's double portraits dominated the fashionable art scene (Isherwood and Bachardy, Henry Geldzahler and Christopher Scott, Mr and Mrs Clark with Percy – this last being the Tate Gallery's most popular painting). They quickly responded to each other's total lack of pretension or guile, and quietly looked upon those conventional folk scurrying busily to impress or to find favour as impoverished souls.

I first knew Wayne independently of Hockney altogether, when he was a seventeen-year-old student about to leave the Royal Ballet School around the corner from me in Baron's Court and launch his ambitious claims to the focused attention of the British public. It was known that I had some empty bedrooms and occasionally offered them to theatrical people as a stepping-off spot before their professional life allowed them independence. So Wayne Sleep was sent to me as a youngster in need of a bed. He stayed about six months; that was all the time it took before his prodigious talent sent him quickly into solo roles at Covent Garden and a premature stardom.

Wayne had been sent to ballet classes as a little boy to correct a malformation – he had been flat-footed, I think – and, as often happens in the mysterious ballet world, an unremarkable medical initiative unlocked a brimming desire to entertain and to sparkle. Once the youngster was on his way, it seemed that nothing would be allowed to stop him, even the uncomfortable fact that he was far too short ever to take the leading male role as prince in any of the great classical ballets. Such was his ambition that he determined to turn this disadvantage on its head. If he could not lord it above the other men in nobility of physique and height, he would beat them by dancing better than any of them. He chose, in fact, to dazzle by technique, and worked so hard that by the time he left school to join the Royal Ballet he was already the only man since Nijinsky who could accomplish an *entrechat huit* (wherein the dancer jumps vertically into the air and criss-crosses his ankles four times before landing again). He soon topped that by executing an *entrechat dix* (ditto, crossing five times), which everybody said had never been done before. He had not been in the Company long before he was cast in solo roles which he quickly mastered so as to make them *his* roles, rendering any competition for them useless. The Mandolin *pas-de-deux* in *Sleeping Beauty*, partnering Lesley Collier or Brenda Last, was one of the first, to be followed by the Jester in *Cinderella*, 'Napoleon' in *Cinderella*, unforgettably funny in a *pas-de-deux* with the choreographer Frederick Ashton, Alain the village idiot in *La Fille Mal Gardée*, and many others.

Even these successes, it turned out, were but a prelude to Wayne's real ambition, which was to star on stage in his own company, dancing not only ballet but tap and jazz. This he achieved before he was thirty, while still being invited back to the Royal Ballet for guest appearances. For a boy from Plymouth with dodgy feet, this was no small achievement.

He was, of course, driven by an unconquerable desire to entertain, to hold the audience in his grip and make them applaud his vast enthusiasm. His addiction to the stage was less a vainglorious enterprise than a pressing need to share, to infect the audience with his own joy and excitement. It worked because it was genuine, and audiences are quick to spot a fraud. Indeed, I don't think they can ever be hoodwinked. Wayne's overwhelming effervescence spilled over into his off-stage life. He was nearly always the last to leave a party, charming and collecting everyone in sight; he was the first to try out the latest suspect substance, and react with delight at its unexpected and often hilarious consequences; and he was sexually not voracious but adventurous, anxious to attempt anything at least once. One was never bored with Wayne's company, but I often wondered if he was perhaps occasionally bored with it himself, whether he had, in fact, a fear of loneliness which might leave him to think thoughts he would rather keep at bay. There was no real evidence for this conjecture, save the positively exhilarating passion of his presence; he abhorred a vacuum, a moment's emptiness, an opportunity for reflection. It suggested overreach of some kind.

As if in recognition of this, Wayne asked me to prepare a reading-list for him. Although ballet schools were obliged by the demands of the national curriculum to provide a general education, this was kept to the strict minimum required, so as to leave the major part of the day to dance. The consequence of such exclusivity was that most dancers were completely un-read, with no knowledge of the classics of literature, and no time (nor, for the most part, inclination) to read the latest novel or biography. Ballet-dancers customarily read the times of class and rehearsal for the following day, and that was it. Wayne was painfully aware of this, and felt short-changed. He wanted to improve himself, to become more literate, I suppose, and I thought this latest ambition of his rather touching, for he would get no applause for it from a public unaware of his endeavour. We started with a list of six books, which he promptly went out and bought, and we would meet every two weeks or so to discuss them. The first, I recall, was William Golding's *Lord of the Flies*, which he questioned with thorough-going logic. But the impetus ran low whenever a new schedule of rehearsals intervened, as it was bound to do.

Wayne's most beguiling quality was his cheekiness. He spoke off-the-cuff, without weighing his words, which meant that many of his remarks were ill-judged, but always amusing, and always forgiven. There was a story, which I cannot vouch-safe as I was not present, that his unquenchable *penchant* for saying whatever came into his head was even let loose on the Queen. He was presented to Her Majesty for the second time and she, with that perfect knack and timing for which she is famous, attempted to put him as his ease by saying, 'We've met before, haven't we?' Without pause for breath, he responded, 'Oh, have we? Where was that?' I do hope it is true. Certainly it is in character.

Wayne, now sixty, and loved by thousands of heavy-drinking pub louts who would normally look upon ballet-dancers with contempt, has in this way achieved something else, namely the spreading of ballet's popularity into corners where it would previously have been unable to penetrate. In some ways this is because the national *mores* have matured beyond the bovine prejudices of the immediate post-war period, but in large part it is also due to Wayne's personality and popularity. The public, too, recognised that he spoke without prevarication, without 'side' or concealed motive, and both respected and loved him for it. He is one of those few entertainers whose own selfhood becomes the ultimate prize that he has to offer the audience. When he famously danced on the Covent Garden stage with a partner twice his height, the Princess of Wales (much to the evident consternation of the Prince), the country cheered him on, not because he was a star but because he was one of them.

Reflecting on the people I have written about in the fore-going pages, I find myself wondering now whether there is any thread which links these disparate characters together in such a way as to justify their appearing together in the same chapter. I have written about them as they occurred to me, without theme or structure, and yet I now see that they are bound by the same description which arguably applies to the subjects of some of my books. That is, they are all mavericks. I am naturally

201

drawn to people who make their own rules and chart their own course independently of conventional expectations, precisely because I can do neither. Each of the writers and painters I have mentioned is self-evidently an original, a man or woman who has opened a door through which nobody has passed before and invited us ordinary mortals to follow if we dare. They have sprung ready-formed from an intuitive well of unsuspected possibilities. My writing, on the other hand, has been competent, interesting and occasionally revelatory, but it is all the result of swotting. I discovered how to do my revision, how to pass exams, how to marshal facts in such a way as to provoke a conclusion, but there is no originality in any of it. The doors I opened were opened by many before me. My route was well-trodden.

Socially as well as professionally, I come to similar conclusions. Hockney, Sleep, Sondheim, and in a rather different manner the Mitford sisters, are all blazingly different from the common-or-garden, placidly pleasant individuals who provide the *dramatis personae* of most narratives and personal biographies. They positively shout with self-assurance, aware of their own sparkle and merit and worth without ever having to display them, peacock-like, for admiration and acclamation. (The obvious exception is Wayne Sleep, since his profession requires he be a peacock, but even he has shown the feathers he wanted to show, not those demanded of him.) I have never had that certainty, that calm knowledge of personal distinction, but have always felt myself to be one of the herd.

I have sat on several committees, but never raised my voice or offered an idea at any of them, for fear of derision. When I speak in public, it has to be rehearsed, lest I say something foolish. Given splendid opportunities, I will not embrace them unless I am sure I will succeed. Faint-heartedness is written into my genes. I have told elsewhere of my six-month hitchhiking venture in the United States, wearing a pin-striped suit and a bowler hat, when I was twenty years old, and the many adventures that led to. I did not mention that one of my rides was offered by a man who turned out to work in the State Department in Washington DC and that he and his wife generously offered me a bed at their house in Maclean, Virginia, a very posh suburb of Washington. One day he took me along to a press conference given by President Kennedy. In those days, presidential press conferences were much less decorous than they are now, and much less stage-managed. The President was plied with questions for which he probably could not have prepared in advance but to which he responded with fluency and charm. There was an easy-going, relaxed, respectful atmosphere, and I was made very welcome by everyone I encountered. The time came when I was invited by the President to proffer a question of my own. I muttered some excuse and shrank into silence. I simply did not dare be heard. No maverick would shy away so timidly. He would speak because it would not occur to him that anyone might not want to hear what he had to say. Those of us who are swots must be sure of their ground before they pipe up.

Perhaps hitchhiking in America dressed like a stockbroker was being a maverick of sorts, but not to any great purpose. Then again, I once walked from London to Brighton, a distance of fifty-three miles, in football boots. An idiotic venture, I now agree, but I was seventeen and, together with other school prefects at Wilson's Grammar, had accepted a wager from younger boys that we could not do such a thing. We agreed on payment of a pittance, augmented by some of the teachers, destined for a charitable concern. There were five of us, shorts, socks, football boots, walking-sticks, ridiculously ill-clad for a deadly ordeal. The walk took seventeen and a half hours. The first of us dropped out before the halfway mark, at Crawley, by which time my feet were squelching with blood from vicious blisters and every step taken required an effort of will. Two of us finished, Bob Moy twenty yards ahead of me, urging me on, me loudly cursing his stubbornness. We collapsed on to the shingles at Brighton, were carefully wrapped in newspaper by local tramps, and rescued by our Latin master, who lived nearby, the following morning. We were taken to hospital, unable to walk for another three days afterwards. Now, was that the act of a brave, self-assertive maverick? Or the fruitless showing-off of a fool? The latter, I am afraid. A boy with original personality would have found a more fitting avenue for adventure, one which had a *point* at least. Pusillanimity in committee is the mirror of empty bravado in public; they are paths that avoid grappling with anything important.

I have been blessed with friendships. People have on the whole been ready to tolerate my lack of courage in return for easy social intercourse, a flow of conversation which rarely flags. I have had (horrible but irreplaceable expression) the 'gift of the gab'. My English teacher at Wilson's, J. A. D. Parr, the man to whom I owe every insight I have ever developed and whose influence I celebrated in *Getting Personal*, noticed the facile traps which awaited me long before I was aware of them. In 1958, soon after I left school, he wrote to me with 'a word of warning':

> You have found that a modest and diffident manner works wonders. Now begin to distrust your own success. You are a master of the contact, but contacts are only superficial – and that is the chief danger to you. Dare to be alone, and to go deep. Undertake what is too difficult at a first encounter. Friends you will always have, but it is a good thing to shut the door at times.

I now marvel at his prescience. At the time I received this

letter, I was too young to appreciate its import. But it is at least possible that I have followed JAD's advice without knowing it (I now reread the letter for the first time in nearly fifty years, having entirely forgotten it). I have treasured friendship, and found it easy to amuse and entertain people who are bigger, brighter, shinier than myself, the very 'mavericks' to whom I keep referring. But I have found the necessary solitude to ponder and 'go deep' in my professional work, thus balancing ebullience and reflection in a way which has surprised even me. The writers I have mentioned have all contributed to literature, which I have not; writers who are drawn to the subject of 'true crime' usually produce sententious rubbish, which I have not. I have found my weight somewhere in between, and have been comfortable with it. If one has to be a 'maverick' in order to soar, then I have been content with my conventional level. And the friends who have neither expected nor demanded any bonus have given me cheer when I have felt downcast, solace when I have felt isolated, and uplift when I have been tempted to bemoan my grey, earthbound self. I wonder if the mavericks can claim as much.

CHAPTER EIGHT

Two Selves

At random, I come across two old photographs of myself. In each one there is an animal. The first was taken at Howletts, John Aspinall's home and private zoo in Kent, when I was researching to write his biography. Part of my job, I felt, was to experience at first-hand the extraordinary closeness he felt to the animals in his care, a closeness entirely at odds with the Englishman's fetish about pets and being loved by them. Aspers with his gorillas or his tigers or his ruffed lemurs was a living creature sharing space with other living creatures, giving and receiving respect and curiosity on a level scarcely comprehended by banal pet-owners. With the big silverback male head of the gorilla family, Aspers was the guest in his house, the visitor to be tolerated only as long as the host required. He submitted to the animal's whims, even if it meant having his eyebrows plucked by a big hairy hand at the end of which were surprisingly delicate fingertips, and joined the gorilla in play. This might involve some rough biting and punching, but the gorilla, who could have killed the man with one stroke of his mighty arm, was never a danger, for they are not aggressive creatures and do not seek to do harm. Indeed, there was once a film of Aspers playing with his first great silverback which, when slowed down, revealed the gorilla containing his strength by deliberately curling his fist before striking, so that what looked like a hefty blow was in reality a gentle brush (in gorilla terms) with the back of his hand. All this was rendered possible by trust, that massive quality which can be defined only in the abstract and which eludes all attempt to demonstrate in language. (Indeed, the moment we begin to convince somebody we are trustworthy, we prove that we are not, for words are meant to explain, and trust withers when explained.)

Having given his trust, and the gorilla or the tiger having accepted it, Aspers then had the right to expect it in return, and I always saw it given in abundance. A tigress who dropped her cubs into his lap, licked him squarely on the jaw, and trotted off into the distance for a much-needed rest, gave eloquent advertisement for this astonishing, and very gratifying togetherness. Most zoo-people before Aspers, forever treating the animals in their care as dangerous beasts to be fed and prodded into obedience, had no inkling that such was possible. Oh dear, what they all missed! I once saw a so-called keeper in Jamaica who entertained visiting tourists by hitting crocodiles on the nose to provoke them into opening their great jaws in protest; I wanted to break his skull. And in India, bears are still routinely tortured and tormented for public fun in spectacles which make me seethe with fury. Thus, in writing *The Passion of John Aspinall* I disappointed a number of folk who wanted the truth about his unhappy first marriage, his friendship with the fugitive Lord Lucan and his persuading of foolish rich young men to lose their millions at his gaming tables. While not ignoring these matters, I concentrated on what made Aspers unique (wives, money and murderers being commonplace); and that was his touch on the pulse of life.

He was not an intellectual, in the sense of academic study, although his reading was wide and his knowledge deeper than that of many an academic. He was closer to Konrad Lorenz, the instinctive animal-student, than to Solly Zuckerman, the empty theoretician. In fact, he heartily despised Zuckerman at a time when it was fashionable to applaud him. Rather than elaborate a scholarly paper on what he discovered about animal behaviour and responses, he would show it and live it. His life was the way he behaved on his estate with his animals, his biography was watchable more than describable. To understand what he was doing, and why he was doing it, one had somehow to do the same, in however tiny a measure.

There was one baby gorilla which had been rescued from certain death in the jungle. His mother had been slaughtered, her hands cut off to be sold as ashtrays to souvenir-hunters. The need for warmth and contact and care is as strong with a gorilla as it is with a human baby or child, and this one would have perished by itself, unless another gorilla family had adopted him. Since he had already been prised out of the jungle into a village, this would have been unlikely. So he was brought to Kent and adopted by Aspers, with a view to introducing him into one of the fully functioning gorilla families already resident there, when the time was ripe. Aspers and his keepers called the orphan Djala.

For the first six months Djala had to be reared by hand, with extreme compassion and attentiveness. Two rooms were prepared for him at the top of the house and one of the female assistant keepers was brought in to share this accommodation with him, she in one room with a bed and wardrobe, he in the adjacent room with his straw and his ropes and his playthings. They started the day together and finished it together, her devotion (quite unsentimental, one must add, for sentiment can send the experiment on an improper detour) giving Djala the feeling of being-in-the-world, of not being isolated and bereft, which he necessarily craved. This is what I meant by Aspers having his finger on the pulse of life. He knew that all life on earth was interconnected in a way established by science but neglected by philosophy (and completely demolished by religion and politics), and that the deepest source of both calm and significance was to accept one's part in this great throbbing web and do nothing to loosen its fragile bonds. A web takes much labour and ingenuity to construct, but it can be destroyed in a second. Unlike some of the people who denigrated him, Aspers was not a destroyer.

When Djala was old and secure enough to live in his own quarters, when he was in fact still a child but no longer an infant, he was moved out of the house and given an enclosure where he could see and hear other gorillas, and where he could be visited by keepers from time to time. I asked whether I might become a regular visitor, having already been introduced to him at the house. He knew me to some extent, and would not be frightened by my sudden arrival in his own space. Thus did I spend countless hours with Djala, sharing much with him, and speaking with eyes and gestures.

Being a vegetarian, a gorilla smells wonderful. I suspect that I, with my meat-eating habits, must have stunk in his nostrils, but he did not reject me on that account. He welcomed me with a grunt and pursed lips and eyes which held a world of meaning in their deep brown reflective quietude. He seemed to be saying, 'What do you propose which could be of interest to me?' or, 'Don't take advantage, I am letting you in as a favour,' or, 'I haven't seen you for a long time, what makes you think I want to now?' All of which is richly anthropomorphic and ridiculous, as I fully realise. It is impossible to know what Djala was thinking, which is why I used the caveat word 'seemed'. But the point of the anthropomorphic approach, though deluded, is to voice the sense of receptiveness in me. I know for certain that he was thinking and feeling something, I could see that working in his eyes, and for want of proof, it was up to me to imagine those thoughts as best I could. Their truth is not in their accuracy, which cannot be ascertained, but in their effect. There was undeniably contact and comprehension of sorts.

The anthropomorphic mistake, of seeing ourselves reflected

in the behaviour of other creatures and attributing to them motives and desires which we might have in their place, is helpful if we turn it back to front and look at the corollary. It was always intuitively obvious, and is now scientifically confirmed, that we can learn very much indeed about human behaviour by watching that of other animals, for ours derives, genetically, historically and socially, from theirs. The origin of what we now call morality lies in the clear choices which speechless and reasonless animals have long made in their dealings with one another. The gorilla who swiped Aspinall but held back his strength so as to do no real harm, made a *choice* so to do, as there was an alternative – namely to thrash him or rip his arm off – which was not taken up. Such a choice cannot be instinctive, it must have evolved through a learning process, and its far more sophisticated descendant is our code of social conduct, and eventually, even, our moral sense.

Thus the truth comes as a passionate shock, that all living creatures are not only fashioned from the same genetic soup, not only share similar DNA profiles, but are a richly interconnected and interdependant family. Something like this has been said in prayers from childhood, more or less by rote, but rarely have its implications been fully taken on board. It means that morality is to be assessed by the acts it condones and condemns, not mitigated or diluted according to the recipient of the act. Cruelty is cruelty whether it is inflicted upon a child or a centipede, an old woman or a young whale. And it must follow from this that any decent human being should support all those maligned organisations devoted to the protection of animals from human viciousness. For if he does not, he is disabling his moral inheritance.

It is unfortunate that most of these organisations talk of Animal Rights, which is a misnomer. Only human societies have invented the notion of rights, and it is slightly absurd to pretend that other animals can lay claim to those abstractions which we have confected for ourselves. No, animals do not have 'rights', but they are manifestations of life, as precious as our own, and we have 'duties' to respect that life. The onus is upon us.

Having seen and smelt the sense of terror in a slaughter-house, the wide terrified eyes of those who know they are about to be killed, the screams of fear, the panic to escape, and the brutality of the slaughterers, I would gladly join any organisation which promised to eradicate such horrors perpetrated in my name, and in yours. I would protest against the barbarous practice of vivisection, done for so-called medical research and quite unnecessary, and, yes, I would punish those who profit from such disgusting livelihoods, personally if the law will not do it for me. If I saw a man bludgeon a baby seal to death, its head burst open in red profusion, while its mother watches and wails hopelessly, I might even grab the club and bludgeon the man's head with it, until it too burst open like a pomegranate. I have heard of kittens being thrust down the waste-disposal unit of a Californian kitchen by bored teenagers looking for a different kind of amusement. I have heard of a cat being thrown alive into the boiling fat of a fish-and-chip shop in England. Is it extremist to want to visit pain upon these cruel, morally vacuous people who bring shame upon us all? Or are they the extremists, the corrupters of our moral compass?

Of course chickens have to be eaten, as everything in life is part of the interdependant cycle. But they do not need to be thrown against the wall, or have their beaks removed, any more than African tribal women need to have their vaginas sewn up to prevent the attentions of men. This is the true message of the anthropomorphic approach, that life is dear and must not be degraded by practices which our species alone is capable of inventing; it reminds one of the circularity of life, and of its shared bounty. We all flourish beneath the same sun. The adage, *Do unto others as you would have others do unto you*, or the precept *Love thy neighbour as thyself*, only achieve full meaning and import when they are seen to apply to the whole of life, and not merely to one species within it.

This is, perhaps, why I have been drawn, intellectually and emotionally, towards Buddhism rather than any theist religious system. As I understand it, the Buddhist philosophy respects all life and will not permit any act which extinguishes it. I have seen an illustration of this at close quarters. In Thailand in 1966 I found myself in conversation with a young Buddhist monk, as we hovered over one of those enterprising cooks in Bangkok who prepare a meal for sale over a small burner on the pavement – no rates, no rent, no overheads! We fell into conversation easily, being both in our twenties, and I quickly worked out that the Thai people are in any case naturally welcoming and gregarious; they do not wait for formal introductions. He invited me to visit his monastery, a big complex of buildings by the mighty, turgid river some way out of the city, with an atmosphere of peace and serenity which it is difficult to convey. It was as if the calm was effortless, natural, not the result of some deprivation of will or imposition of rule as in many a European monastery. Indeed, when my host took me to meet his friends, they were a bunch of some twenty young men quite as hearty as one would expect to find anywhere, ready to joke and laugh at each other's rough grappling with the English language (for my sake), eager to learn about the Queen and various football stars, full of mirth and mischief. Had they not all been clad in orange robes, they might have been on a street corner in Guildford. But they had a mystifying air of lyrical purity and peace about them, as if even gossip, in their hands, could only be harmless. I recall one of them being teased by the others for effeminacy, yet peculiarly without any hint of menace.

They insisted that they wash me, as the most ennobling gift they could offer a guest. I was duly hidden by a vast sheet while they poured jugs and jugs of water over me, then wrapped me and dried me in an act of cleansing which was obviously designed to be utterly selfless and charitable. It, too, was a domestic ceremony which carried no baggage of threat; I am almost embarrassed that it should be necessary to clarify, as if I were letting them down by explanation, that there was nothing of the lewd or bawdy in their generosity. Duly washed, I was then taken into the temple to be presented to the chief monk, and instructed on the correct form of salutation, on my knees, my head pressed to the ground. The venerable elder announced a formal gesture of welcome to me, the stranger, and turning directly to me, with the sound of the river as gentle background accompaniment, he spoke in Thai, which my friend immediately translated. His words were, 'May the happinesses of your life follow one another as sequentially and naturally as do the ripples on the surface of the water.' Simple maybe, but I do not think I have ever felt so flattered by the attention of words. This was the disembodied love of men for mankind, or, more than that, the expression of a pagan desire for well-being.

Back in the young men's cell, we sat on the bare floor, with no comfort to mollify, no 'things' to get in the way of our communication with one another. There were, of course, also ants on the floor, and they soon began to crawl over my feet and legs, then my arms. Not many, but sufficient to alarm a fastidious and spoilt Englishman. The young Thais saw my anxiety, and with smiles breaking into giggles, came to my rescue. They carefully picked off each one of the dozen or so creatures and placed them back on the floor where they belonged. None was crushed or concussed. Is it any wonder I left that place feeling rather abashed, somewhat ashamed of the times I had thoughtlessly squashed the breath out of a tiny vessel of the planet's plenitude of life, or thoughtlessly treated a person to less than the full flush of respect and affection that his being alive merits. And the conflation of the two within the same sentence is what really matters. For the moment you regard the ant as inferior your potential for spiritual understanding is lost.

It is interesting that the three great Western religions which evolved in what we now call the Middle East have all been violent and life-insulting. Judaism, Christianity and Islam all have blood on their hands, not by accident but because they are all anthropocentric, arrogant and unreflective. Their violent histories are not aberrations but inevitabilities, sewn in the seeds of their restricted vision. If moral behaviour is to be grounded in 'winning' and 'victory' and 'glory', and the entire rest of the sentient world to be utterly shut out from a system which regards man as the only value, then it is not surprising that these religions become bereft of spiritual content. We admit as much in our vocabulary, but rarely acknowledge it. We talk glibly of 'Christian soldiers', 'chosen people', 'Muslim fundamentalists', without noticing that the first is a paradox, the second an arrogation, the third a question begged. Yet we tacitly accept that terrorists can be Jewish, Muslim or Christian (and historically have been all three), because it is in the nature of those religions to spawn and encourage intolerance. Now if we ask ourselves why we never hear of a Buddhist terrorist, we are unlikely to investigate further for fear of the uncomfortable truth we may uncover. A Buddhist terrorist is unthinkable – an oxymoron if ever there was one.

Hence the fashionable denigration of the young who, from the 1960s onwards, joyously embraced Eastern philosophies which, they discovered, did not enjoin them to conquer and destroy. With palpable relief a generation of hopeful idealists escaped from their dreadful, deadening disillusion with the starkly materialistic values of the West and found gentleness and wisdom in oriental teachings. Of course, they did not understand it all. Neither do I. I have tried to grapple with the intricacies of Buddhist philosophy, with those elusive notions of impermanence and awareness, of suffering and 'voidism', but have generally penetrated as deep as a pin-prick; the fanciful and amusing constructions of Bishop Berkeley (according to whom a table is not there unless you are looking at it) are far more accessible. But the essence of the Buddha does not depend upon epistemological abstractions. He demonstrated that there was a route to calm through concentration away from the self, that decency in social intercourse, clarity in moral thinking, and universal friendliness and compassion *necessarily* eradicated selfish behaviour and thought, because they banished all cravings, which are always cravings for the self. Cravings for happiness, for wealth, for success, for sexual pleasure, for applause, are all antithetical to spiritual life and enchain the individual to avoidable suffering. Kindness and thinking in an outward direction produce calm, which is not so much contentment as the expulsion of poison. What excited young Europeans and Americans about these ideas was that they were utterly democratic, available to anyone irrespective of family, income, skin colour or academic achievement. You simply had to concentrate.

And, to return to my original point, the Buddha made clear that right-thinking and moral cleanness applied to our behaviour *vis-à-vis* all living creatures, that it was impossible to be calm and at peace and at the same time cruel, whatever the object of the cruelty, for it was the cruelty itself which was wrong and literally upsetting. 'All men tremble at punishment,' the Buddha said, 'all men fear death. Likening others to oneself, one should neither slay nor cause to slay.'

It says much, I fear, about the bankruptcy of Western moral

thought that when one hears a great Western lament, such as Britten's transcendent *War Requiem*, it is not to Jesus or Moses or the Prophet Mohammed that the mind turns, but to the gentle Buddha (though I am sure Jesus, had he known of the man from the East who preceded him by five centuries, would have hailed him as a brother). The *War Requiem* is an anguished cry of remorse for the miserable slaughter of millions of young men, scarcely out of their adolescence, in the mud of Europe during the First World War. It interweaves the Latin mass, with all the usual inclusions of *Dies Irae, Agnus Dei, Rex Tremendae, Lacrimosa* and *Libera Me*, with the poems of Wilfred Owen, poignantly decrying 'the pity of war, the pity of war distilled'. These poems are sung, separately, and the final one together, by a tenor and baritone, the tenor representing the British soldier, the baritone the German, while the Latin mass is celebrated by a soaring soprano. The world première in 1962 was performed in the newly rebuilt Coventry Cathedral, with huge symbolism, for this Gothic marvel had been destroyed by German bombers in the Second World War and reconstructed partly with the help of young German volunteers. Of course, the occasion was by invitation only, in the presence of the Queen. But I attended a public performance in London a little while later.

The English tenor was Peter Pears, the German baritone Dietrich Fischer-Dieskau, and the soprano, with a voice ascending as high and overwhelming as a Gothic spire itself, was the Russian Galina Vishnevskaya. Thus were the three great historical adversaries and glorifiers of war, and also those that suffered most from it, represented by a performer from each country. The weight of this choice was not lost upon the audience, and at the moment the tenor sings Owen's line, 'I am the enemy you killed, my friend', to no musical accompaniment whatever, Britten having silenced his trumpets, strings, drums and choirs for that solitary, fleeting moment, the hall held its breath. The moment may have been fleeting, but its effect lingered, and the audience, moreover, willed it to linger. The pity of war, indeed.

More than forty years later, I heard this tremendous work again, at the Royal Albert Hall, with an American soprano fittingly singing the mass in the aftermath of the American conquest of Iraq, which produced thousands of needless deaths to the satisfaction of heartless politicians. Perhaps because of this circumstance, the performance was yet more powerful and resonant. Colin Davis conducted with passion and commitment; it seemed the choir spoke for all of us, Davis channelling our feelings as well as theirs. And as the Requiem drew to its peaceful close, after the two soldiers have together sung 'Let us sleep now', the choir's collective voice did not merely grow softer, quieter, slower, it seemed to evaporate into the ether, not quite coming to an end, but continuing on elsewhere, somewhere, for ever. At that moment the entire auditorium froze. Not a movement, not a cough, not an intake of breath, not a shuffle of feet, nothing but solid, total silence, for what must have been up to two minutes. Nobody instructed us, nobody expected it, the three singers appeared stunned by it, the conductor bowed his head before it, and the choir was visibly chastened by it. Why? Because unquestionably we were all, performers and audience alike, thinking of those First World War boys, dead and gone for nothing, in homage and sadness. This must have been what Britten intended. It enveloped us all. And my point is, however far-fetched it may appear in dry print on a page, that we were none of us Christian at that moment: we were Buddhist.

*   *   *

If the Buddhist ideal resides in clear, sequential thinking towards the resolution of conflict and its replacement by peace;

in authentic feeling conducive to circumstances which promote this peace; and in energy directed outwards, away from the self; then I suppose I have been inclined towards Buddhism all my life without knowing it to be so. I have thought that it was a kind of honest Christianity to which I aspired, one closely attuned to Jesus's own pacific and tolerant humanity, but the Christian church which inherited his name and exploited his reputation, and which he would have roundly deplored, has concentrated far too much on the satisfaction of personal desire – especially for bliss in eternity – to hold any real value. The Buddhist ambition to achieve freedom from personal desires is much more sound, philosophically and ethically.

You measure your behaviour mostly in your relations with others, with animals, as I have said above, as with humans. And especially when looking at close personal relationships one can discern immediately whether or not the ideals have been achieved. Alas, almost every examination will reveal that they have not, so powerful a drive is the Self, so insatiable and destructive. There have been few real saints in the world, as I ruefully realised in writing the last chapter of *The Evil That Men Do*, when I could barely muster half a dozen of them. And yet, surely, we must all *intend* to do good and encourage happiness when we enter into a relationship, we cannot mean to visit pain and torment upon our family and lovers from the outset, unless, that is, we are pathologically perverse. I have written enough about some such people in my time to know that they are extremely rare. Most of us make a mess of things through mere incompetence, born of an inability properly to interpret the actions of others through the distorting prism of the Self. The Self gets in the way, it obtrudes, it trips you up, it discolours and diverts, it is like a solid wall of black basalt blotting out the truth, which nevertheless remains there, teasingly perceptible, just out of reach.

I let my mother down by failing to show love in a whole-hearted way, free of embarrassment. She was seriously deaf most of her life, and in the last ten years virtually imprisoned in a silent world. I learnt, obviously, to speak clearly and directly at her, so that she could work things out by a combination of lip-reading and intuition (she told me she fashioned her face to match that of her interlocutor, hoping a tiny laugh or a sorrowful look might be appropriate), but this was merely strategically helpful. Far too often I embellished the performance by shouting at her, not angrily at all, but, perhaps worse, mockingly, addressing myself to the top of her head where I suspected the microphone of her hearing device might be concealed. I thought all this was cheerful-chappie nonsense, and that she would appreciate my sense of fun. I dimly recall even reasoning that it was far better for her to have me turn the affliction into a joke, thereby ridding it of its sting. How wrong I was. It remained an affliction, added to the many she endured in a lifetime ruined by illness of one kind of another, and she had a right to expect more compassion from me. She never complained (she was one of the half-dozen 'saints' I celebrated in the book mentioned above), but she did once gently point out to me that I should above all look after my health: 'If you have good health, Brian, nothing else matters so much.' I wondered why that admonition stuck in my memory so tenaciously for more than thirty years. It was, after all, a simple remark, in the midst of one ordinary afternoon. But I think I was struck by the seriousness of her tone, by her need to say something, for once, that I would listen to in earnest. It was probably after I had been comically shouting at her hair.

This was important because my Self intruded and prevented me from behaving towards my mother in a way that would have brought her peace and a harmonious ease. It intruded by way of a concern about my own embarrassment which pre-vented me from expressing my love for her, and moreover deep gratitude to her, in an unEnglish demonstrative fashion that might have made me wince, but instead had me so disguising it in humour that it was barely recognisable as affection at all. Once, when she was weak and her breathing was poor, I arrived in Wales to visit her and found her asleep on top of the bed. I was able to hold her hand as she woke up to find me there. Odd to think that I had never done it before, that I had waited almost to the end before being a son to her.

When my brother Colin and I accepted that she should move into a hospice for cancer patients, at least for a while, where she could be looked after properly, I think she was relieved. She went in one afternoon, and died that same night. I think she went because she knew she would no longer be a nuisance to us both.

My father was quite a different matter. I failed him by not acknowledging his crippling shyness and low self-esteem, which were so severe that they reduced him to a helpless stutter in every conversation, and especially in those where he was trying to admonish me. I was cleverer than he, and made him suffer with the knowledge of it. He was clearly proud of me, and instead of accepting this, a real if oblique expression of love, I reminded him of how little pride he engendered in those around him. I scornfully and cruelly dismissed his admittedly crude opinions, when I could so easily have asked him to explain them. He would have been flattered and pleased. As it was, his son was his tormentor. I do not recall this with any relish, and it needs no elucidation to see how the Self I held so precious was here the provoker of pain and discord. I could not see it at the time. Had I been able to, I would have been ashamed.

My brother Colin, too, had the misfortune to be close as my

young adolescence sprang into its arrogant strut. I teased him without mirth, and this bewildered him. I could have helped him grow into maturity as I became a young man, and I believe I felt that I was doing so by treating him at school without that bias of affection which he might have expected. But in truth I was demonstrating to myself, and to anyone else who cared to be looking, that I was above considering the unfair links of family, and in so doing I damaged a boy's self-image and trust. He must have hated me for a while.

And so it goes on, the stumbling meandering race through life, blindly in pursuit of what one thinks are the best purposes, unknowingly sewing seeds for the worst harvest. If there were a God, I should like to be able thank him for the rehearsal, and tell him I am now ready for the actual performance. For it is only when one has lived life that one knows, dimly, how it ought to be lived. Too late. I do envy those Buddhist boys who are taught the wisdom of age while the ignorance of youth still hangs over them.

I was once berated by a critic for being too 'abject', and I can feel that same self-pity creeping into these paragraphs as I write. So let me say that there have been some connections in my life which have not been calamitous, wherein I have striven to do right and have on the whole succeeded. My friendship with Jean-Philippe in France did him nothing but good and left him with no scars. Perhaps we were lucky, in that my desire for transient happiness coincided with his. For though he was only a lad of sixteen, he had enough common-sense to realise that these intense feelings were for now, not for ever, and that it would be mad to behave as if they were anything more. So he grabbed the moment and enjoyed it. Very French, that. An English boy in similar circumstances would have been crippled by anxieties.

It has sometimes been suggested that I am masochistic by

nature, a charge I have always found incomprehensible. I have, undeniably, shown an aptness to attract, as a magnet does iron filings, the most difficult, destructive and disturbed people to nest in my shadow, but I have never *enjoyed* the dramas provoked by their behaviour. That is not to say, of course, that I have not subconsciously invited them, for reasons I do not begin to understand. And this is where the self-examination becomes severely uncomfortable. For I have begun dipping into early diaries which I kept from 1966 until about 1983, and which I have not seen since they were written. I did not consult them, thank God, for *Getting Personal*, as they were locked in a bank vault. The book might well have turned out significantly different had I taken them out. For the person they reveal is quite a stranger to the person who has been writing these present pages.

I have been, rather too proudly perhaps, advocating the need to suffocate the Self and embrace the Buddhist notion of harmlessness. I have meant every word, and would repeat it all if required. I have also noted that I have been called 'abject' and 'masochistic': the one I dimly recognise, the other I totally reject. But what do I find tapped out on an old typewriter by a man who should have been in his early maturity, aged from twenty-seven onwards? Wretchedly self-centred, craven, pitiful stuff, rivers of words dedicated to how miserably I was treated by everyone to whom I became close, symphonies of supine wailing, and a risible, pathetic desire to be lusted after. It is very embarrassing indeed. But it must be true. The person I am now looks at the person I was then, and is utterly appalled. No wonder James Lees-Milne called his autobiography *Another Self*; there could not be a better title for the odd fellow lurking in those alien pages.

Having relied professionally upon archive material for many of my books, I naturally deplore the desire of some people to destroy letters, to interfere, in fact, with the historical evidence. One instance in particular frustrated me. I was the first person to consult the original letters exchanged between Georgiana, wife of the 5th Duke of Devonshire, and Lady Elizabeth Foster, his mistress. These people notoriously lived together in a *ménage à trois* which was both happy and fruitful, and there are descendants of both ladies thriving today. It had always been a mystery why Georgiana was prepared to tolerate this arrangement, and more, why she regarded Lady Elizabeth as her best friend, the one person she adored above all others. Their letters are eloquent testaments to their profound affection, and ought reliably to provide whatever evidence was needed to clarify the nature of their bond. But they do not, for one good reason; after Georgiana's death certain words, sentences, even paragraphs, were blacked out. I took a sample of the letters to the laboratory at New Scotland Yard in an attempt to recover their secrets, and was advised that, since the same ink was used for the blacking out as had been used for the original writing, infra-red technology would not yield any result. Georgiana and Bess kept their secrets.

And why not? I can guess what was being hidden. It is known that Georgiana Spencer had been married to the Duke as a dynastic bargain, it being expected that she would learn to love him. It is also known that she could not get pregnant for many years, or miscarried, and was becoming desperate (the production of an heir was, after all, the initial purpose of the marriage). It is further known that Lady Elizabeth ('Bess') was flirtatious, experienced, sensual. Just look at her portrait by Reynolds, still hanging at Chatsworth, and all these qualities are manifest. I suspect that Georgiana acceded to the affair between her friend and her husband because the friend had given her some very useful practical tips on how better to arouse his interest. It is significant, to say the least, that one clue not scrubbed out by Bess was a reference by her to Georgiana's first-born in the sentence, 'Kiss *our* child for me,' urging Georgiana not to forget her contribution. I think it reasonable to suggest that Bess helped her friend by means of her own superior erotic expertise.

I also think it reasonable, now, that if this were the case, Bess should subsequently erase all written clues in letters between the three friends which might allow us to pry and understand better. Why should we want to? And why should she permit us to? These are private matters, of no historical import, the revelation of which would embarrass their ghosts needlessly.

Hence I now have an urge to consign some of my early diaries to the flames. In the first place, as I am not an historical or social figure, nothing there disclosed could be of the slightest interest, above prurience. And my ghost would certainly be tormented at the thought somebody might read them. My brother? My nieces?

The man depicted therein is not the reasonable, cautious and incipiently wise old fellow who started this chapter. He is a creature swamped and shipwrecked by every emotional relationship he enters into, awash with passion and, when the relationship founders, as it must when rooted in such aggrieved intensity of feeling, first petulant, then devastated in misery. He positively relishes the suffering which is poured upon him; not enjoys, for the suffering is real enough, but acknowledges with abandon. Why else should he turn to his typewriter at the end of every day and tell it what pains he is passing through? Because they mattered to him more than anything else, they justified his existence, they defined him, they showed him what he deserved. Nary a mention is made of museums visited, of political events observed, and the only social happenings, namely dinner-parties he has arranged, are there to display names of people invited, and to measure how much they impinge upon *him*. He imagines, far too easily, that people have been, or are about to be, in love with him, perhaps as a necessary prelude to those disasters which are bound to come and which can fill a score more pages of anguish. He is guilty of a possessiveness which must have been thoroughly suffocating, and moreover deeply irritating, forever asking intimate questions the answers to which he knows are going to be like knives of flame, demanding to know, to be told, deliberately placing himself in a position which will wrack his soul and bring tears of grief. (In this I can see my father towards the end of his life, when he went through a period of madness, suspecting my mother of infidelity, watching her every move, telephoning her every half an hour, and insisting she keep the curtains closed so nobody could look in and see her.) The man of these diaries is a disgustingly immature and shameful person, and it is amazing to me now that he was not told to pull himself together by his temperate friends. It can only be because they felt for him the pity which he had been trying to earn. How ghastly.

He is also a man obsessed with sexual adventure. While professing to know all about love, and to feel it in deeper doses than the rest of mankind, he expresses it by use of the common word for coition, showing that his imagination is tormented not by the loss of somebody's affection and presence, but by his being sexually possessed by somebody else. No wonder good marriages are not based upon lust. He also goes out in search of solace with commonplace and anonymous encounters, and admits as much to the diary, without blush. This is the sort of ugly nonsense that I want to empty from its box and scatter to distant destruction, for were anyone to read it, they would get too accurate an idea of the man that was me. And I do not want to be that man in perpetuity.

Which raises the question, wherein lies the truth? As a writer

I am able to recreate the past in the third person, using my own character and thoughts as my archive, and present them gift-wrapped to the reader. The diarist of 1968 and of 1971 is raw and wounded, unprotected by the tidy analysis of hindsight and denied the dignity of emollient prose. Perhaps both are true, the vulnerable egoist of the diaries, and the reflective urbanity of the old man, and to offer only one of them as the Real Thing would be to bury the reality of the other. The ruminative and measured man I am now is just as valid as the nasty sensualist I was then, drawn in moments of crisis. To contemplate only *him* would be a disservice to me. And I am justified in obliterating the evidence of his emptiness of soul, I think. It is nobody's business but mine, and it is deeply private.

This is why Proust's involuntary memory is so much more reliable than a detailed contemporary account which is a record of mood. The mood cannot be summoned at will, and all the words which record it will seem like so much collapsed, decaying masonry. It is a smell, or a taste, or a touch of the sunset upon a hill, that bring streaming into the view of the mind the person one was when these transient sensations were first experienced. Then you will find truth, both deeper and simpler than the written explanations of what transpired. And when those explanations come dipped in hysteria and histrionic excess, truth does not really get a chance to come up for air.

So destruction it will be.

Index